Embrace
the Infinite

The Science of Spirituality

Embrace
the Infinite

The Science of Spirituality

Anthony Mannucci

BOOKS

Winchester, UK
Washington, USA

First published by O-Books, 2012
O-Books is an imprint of John Hunt Publishing Ltd., Laurel House, Station Approach,
Alresford, Hants, SO24 9JH, UK
office1@o-books.net
www.o-books.com

For distributor details and how to order please visit the 'Ordering' section on our website.

ISBN: 978 1 84694 873 2

A CIP catalogue record for this book is available from the British Library.

Design: Stuart Davies

Printed in the UK by CPI Antony Rowe
Printed in the USA by Offset Paperback Mfrs, Inc

We operate a distinctive and ethical publishing philosophy in all
areas of our business, from our global network of authors to
production and worldwide distribution.

CONTENTS

This book is dedicated to my wife and three children
who make it all worthwhile.

What We Want

The Purpose of This Book

The purpose of this book is to describe how human spirituality can thrive in the modern scientific world. A basic scientific understanding of the world leads naturally to a greater spiritual understanding. Science and spirituality are not in conflict. This is fortunate, because in this modern scientific world we yearn for a deeper spiritual connection.

My hope is that the truths revealed in this book will inspire you. I do not avoid the idea of absolute truth. In this modern multifaceted world it has become commonplace to suggest that all knowledge and values are subjective. I will show why this is not so. A spiritual awakening awaits those who embrace the fundamental truths of this world. I wish to illuminate the path towards that awakening.

The Human Quest for Life's 'Meaning'

Everyone wants their lives to have a sense of purpose or meaning. Nobody wants to believe that their life is useless and serves no purpose. For many people, their religion or their God is intimately connected to their sense of purpose. Many believe that their ultimate purpose in life is to serve God. For others, a sense of purpose comes from their work life or their worldly possessions. Purpose can also come from pursuit of a distant goal, such as to climb a tall mountain. Life's purpose influences our decisions and actions every day. Most of the time, we aren't even aware of how we are motivated by our goals. We don't think about it too much. We just go about our business.

What Does Science Have to Do with Life's Meaning?

Why is a scientist writing a book about life's meaning and its ultimate purpose? What has science to do with any of that? Those are good questions. You will learn from this book that science can lead us towards a renewed sense of purpose and meaning.

How can this be? Can scientific understanding of the natural world tell us anything about life's meaning? Yes it can, but we have to think about things in a new way. This book is a guide towards that new understanding.

Let's begin with the simple things, such as morning and night. Many years ago, in the pre-scientific era, there were many different ideas about how morning and night came to be. For example, the Egyptians believed that God created day and night by the use of two great dome-shaped lights in the sky, the brighter light present during daytime and the dimmer light responsible for nighttime.

Now, science has taught us that what the Egyptians believed is really a myth and not the truth. Now we know that day and night arise due to a spinning earth. Daytime is when the part of the earth we are on rotates 'into the light' to face the sun. Nighttime happens when that part of the earth we are on rotates away from the sun. It's easy to understand now! Our scientific understanding of day and night is simpler than the Egyptian myth in some ways, because we only need one light (our sun), not two.

Day and night provide just one example of a natural phenomenon. What exactly is a 'natural phenomenon'? Something you have probably never thought about since you were a child is that the sequence of day and night is very repeatable and predictable. We usually don't think about nature's repeatability because we expect it. We might go to bed at night wondering what we will feel like in the morning, or whether we will make it through the night. But hardly anyone wonders: 'Will the sun rise tomorrow?' If you were to bring this up in front of friends, colleagues, or at a scientific meeting, you would be laughed at. Everyone knows that the sun will rise tomorrow, because the earth keeps spinning. Short of a catastrophic hit by another planet, the earth will continue to spin, as it has done, for millions more years, and the sun will be there to rise as it has always done.

The purpose of this simple example is to remind us of something profound: the repeatability of nature. Whatever your religion, or even if you are not religious at all, you've noticed an orderliness and repeatability within the natural world. This order and repeatability are 'objective' facts. Everyone is aware of them. What you will learn in this book is that the repeatability of nature contains a message for us. That message is that there is something outside of ourselves that transcends us. The word 'transcend' means 'to rise above' or 'go beyond'. The natural world transcends us by proceeding along its path without us. Nature displays order and repeatability that, as far as we know, will never end.

I stated that the repeatability of nature is 'profound'. Why? Because it speaks of eternity. The repeatability and regularity of our natural world evokes in us an idea of the eternal. Later in this book, I will describe how science has discovered another idea from within the natural world: the idea of 'perfection'. Scientists have discovered that the fundamental building blocks of our world are perfectly formed. More will be said about that later.

So, from nature we learn two ideas: the idea of eternity and the idea of perfection. These ideas are profound to us, because they stand out so singularly from our everyday lives. Although our lives are filled with change, and disorder, and cycles of happiness and strife, we are nevertheless aware of something more ideal. The ideals of eternity and perfection that we can glimpse from nature will inspire us. From that inspiration comes a renewed sense of meaning. That is one way that nature and science can help us find meaning.

Why We Want Meaning: Value

There are many ways to find meaning in our lives, but it is often a struggle. Our belief in meaning is tested at every turn, by misfortunes that befall us or by a sense of futility that can envelop us. If we will all eventually die, what is the point of achieving something good in our lives? Everything we are will come to an end.

Let's focus on this struggle: our urge to find meaning and purpose even though it is not obvious or easy. Everyone searches for a sense of meaning in different ways and to different degrees. I must admit that most of the time, I am not concerned with it. Most of the time, I am thinking about the details in my life, such as what to have for dinner or why my spouse is angry with me, or something related to work. But my sense of meaning is absolutely important to me, even though much of the time I am not thinking about it. When my sense of meaning is challenged, I react ferociously.

The search for meaning is related to the idea of 'value'. We seek meaning because we value our lives and we value what we do with our lives. We value life itself. If we did not value our lives then we would not bother with finding meaning in it.

We believe in value and we seek meaning. Where does this idea of value, of life being 'worth it', come from? Can it come from the natural world? Earlier, I said that studying the natural world, particularly by science, can provide a new sense of meaning. Meaning and value are tied together. Can learning about the natural world help us find a value to living and a sense of purpose in life? I believe it can. That is an important subject of this book.

It is a profound fact that we seek out the meaning of our lives. Each of us believes that our life has value. What does that say about us? Why does it matter to us? To answer that, an idea of who we are is needed.

Uniquely Human: The Search for Meaning

I want to focus on a simple idea: the idea that we understand what meaning is. This sounds simple, but I am trying to focus on an aspect of being human that is taken for granted: our ability to understand the concept of 'meaning'. We could not search for it if we did not understand it. So nearly all of us have that ability to understand there is such a thing as meaning, and that we are connected to it. I suggest to you that this fact alone is important and profound.

Our desire to find meaning in our lives is a profound turning point in our lives. As children, we are mostly not aware of or concerned with this. At some point in our development, it happens: a thought that life has a meaning and it should make sense to us, that there should be a purpose and that things have value. Fundamentally, the notion of value and meaning is an *idea*.

We live and breathe and labor in a world of *ideas*. As humans, we have a very special relationship to ideas: they affect us profoundly. I don't just mean this in the sense of lofty ideals, or something that philosophers are worried about. Ideas get to the core of what we are. Everyone has a relationship to ideas. Even the most emotional, intuitive, perhaps artistic or even hateful individual has ideas and responds to them.

Nature and Ideas
So far in this book, we have discussed these two basic things. *Nature*, or the natural world, is also called the 'material world'. It's what a scientist calls the 'physical world'. This world exists outside of us, consisting of objects and things that you can touch and see. There is also the world of *ideas*, such as the idea of meaning and purpose to life. These two worlds are very different. Later in the book, we will relate them. In relating the material world and the world of ideas we will make the connection between science and spirituality.

Make no mistake about it: the world of ideas is completely different from the material world. Yet, its existence is very real. We as humans have a very strong connection to the world of ideas. We also have a strong connection to the material world. That is why we need to eat food (real, material food made of atoms and molecules)!

Do we also need to 'eat' something from the world of ideas? I suggest we do. To be human, we need to be fed by ideas. We cannot be human without ideas. (Luckily, ideas are free, unlike food.)

Science has the material world as its object of interest. It turns out that science also needs ideas. A central feature of this book is the connection that science makes between the natural world and the world of ideas. We'll discuss this later in the book, but for now, I can start by explaining the *scientific view of what ideas are*.

Science makes the connection between the material world and the world of ideas through this fact: science views human beings as material things. Humans also possess ideas. That is how science makes the connection between the world of ideas and the material world.

The scientific view of ideas is that *ideas* exist as *patterns* in the brains of those who have the idea. I realize that this notion may be hard to grasp. I will explain what this means later in the book. I will also discuss what the implications are. For now, please accept my suggestion that science bridges the world of ideas and the material world through the notion that ideas exist in the brains of people (the 'material' brain that we all have right inside our heads). Ideas don't exist as a material thing that you can weigh or look at. *Ideas are patterns in the physical structure of the brain.* That is the scientific view. Later in the book, we will discuss what we mean by *pattern*. We will find there is an intriguing connection between patterns and our brain.

2

An Absolute Truth

The science of spirituality is founded on a bedrock of truth. In this chapter, I will explain what that truth is. I am so certain of this truth that I call it 'absolute': the Absolute Truth. As you will soon learn, science relies heavily on the Absolute Truth. Understanding the Truth will also bring you spiritual fulfillment. I will do my best to make that connection clear. Science and spirituality are therefore linked by this Truth.[1] The Absolute Truth is that the material world (nature, the physical world) is governed by 'natural law'. We will be referring to 'natural law' many times in this book, so we'll give it its own unique name. We'll call it *Vahhd*. It's very important that you understand what 'governed by natural law' or 'ruled by *Vahhd*' means, so I will explain this very carefully.

When we say that the world is governed by natural law, we are saying something about the 'dynamic' world. The dynamic world is material things in motion or transformation. When something moves or changes form or shape (for example when a car crashes or an explosive detonates), those changes happen under a precise and never-changing set of rules. Material things are always changing. How they change and what makes them change is governed by a set of rules that never change. That set of rules is called 'natural law' or *Vahhd*.

Most people firmly believe in *Vahhd*. It is the very basis of our technological world, whether the technology is primitive (like the wheel, or a spear) or the technology is advanced (like a television or computer). If *Vahhd* did not rule, technology would not work at all (admittedly, it doesn't always work even now!). *Vahhd* is the reason that, when we turn on our television, it starts to work. *Vahhd* is the reason that a spear will pierce the skin of a beast and bring that beast down. *Vahhd* is why objects fall to the ground (every time, every single time). We rely on *Vahhd* every day to live our lives. *Vahhd* is why the sun rises every morning and sets every night.

The Absolute Truth is that *Vahhd* exists and governs the material world. Science has an intimate relationship to *Vahhd*. The job of a scientist is to discover *Vahhd*, to discover the rules that govern the movements and transformations of the material world. Scientists must believe in *Vahhd* to do their job. As we shall see, that belief is profound. Scientists must also believe that *Vahhd* is everywhere, governs all material things, and is eternally present. *Vahhd* never 'turns off' or abandons this world. Science depends on the fact that *Vahhd* is always with us.

What exactly is *Vahhd*? How does it work? Why is it there? How can we know *Vahhd*? In this chapter we will talk about *Vahhd* and some of its characteristics. One of the most profound and awe-inspiring characteristics of *Vahhd* is that, as far as we can tell, *Vahhd* can be described with the language of 'logic'. Logic is fundamental to *Vahhd* and profoundly connected to it. Over the last few hundred years, scientists have learned this lesson over and over again. In this chapter we will discuss logic and *Vahhd* and learn some truly amazing things that you may not have realized.

Before further discussing *Vahhd*, let's discuss logic.

Logic

We all know the word 'logic', and we think we know what it means. What, exactly, is logic? Why is logic so important to understanding the material world?

An important connection between logic and *Vahhd* is through mathematics. You may have forgotten this, or wanted to forget: math is a form of logic. Mathematical logic may appear different from the logic you are most familiar with, but they are really the same thing. As you probably know, scientists have found that mathematical laws describe the material world. Scientists cannot avoid using math to describe that world. Engineers use math every day as they design new machines that behave to their specifications. These machines work because of the constant presence of natural law. If you deal with the material world at a detailed and powerful level, you've got to 'do the math'. Math is just a sophisticated form of logic.

In this chapter I will discuss the 'miraculous' fact that *Vahhd* is governed by logical rules. *The material world obeys logic.* As scientists believe, *Vahhd* obeys logical rules each and every minute of each and every day in every corner of the universe. The logical rules are everywhere and always, eternal. We will see how amazing this really is. *Praise be to Vahhd!*

I still haven't told you what logic *is*. The best way to explain logic is with some simple examples. Let's start with an everyday example: returning movies to a video store. Suppose you know you need to return three movies. You rented one comedy and two dramas. You have two dramas in hand and you are looking for the third movie to return. What type of movie are you looking for? A comedy of course. Logic allows you to figure that out. Even this simple example allows me to make a point about logic: its power to transform ideas. A logical view of this example goes something like this.

A) I have rented three movies: two dramas and a comedy. (Premise 1)

B) I have already found two movies and they are both dramas. (Premise 2)

C) The missing movie is a comedy.

Let's break this down some more: I know two things, called 'premises' in logic-speak. Premise A is 'The three movies are two dramas and a comedy.' Premise B is 'I have two dramas in hand.' Using logic, I can state another truth that is not directly stated in the first two premises: 'The remaining movie is a comedy.' Statements A and B, taken together, can be viewed as immediately

implying statement C: 'The missing movie is a comedy.' This impli-
cation is very powerful and iron clad. I've chosen a simple example
so that there can be no debate about the matter. Statement C must
be true if statements A and B are true. In the world of logic, we
would say that statements A and B together are 'logically equivalent' to statement C. That means that in logical arguments, you can
substitute A and B everywhere you have the statement C, and vice
versa: everywhere you see statement C you can also say it the long
way by repeating statements A and B. If we dared to write an
equation, we could write it as:

A and B implies C

OR

Statement A AND statement B = Statement C

Here's another way to look at it: *transformation*. I start with two
statements and end up with a third, using principles of logic. I've
transformed the two statements A and B into one statement that
'means the same thing'. Although statements A and B are *logically
equivalent* to statement C, they are not the same statement in a
comprehensive sense. Statements A and B use more words, have
different meanings etc., but *logically they are the same*. By the process
of logical deduction, I have been allowed to transform one thing
into another. The statements A and B, taken together, are not the
same thing as statement C. Logic lets me equate them. Equating
means transformation.[2]

Let's get back to the material world. As we said, scientists have
discovered that the material world can be described by mathematics, and mathematics is really just a form of logic. The natural
world obeys logical rules, and logical rules imply transformation.
So we've discovered something very, very profound and important:
Vahhd works by transformation. *Motion* is the transformation of an
object at one location into an object at a different location. Nature
moves and is dynamic by virtue of these transformations. These

transformations occur all around us, all the time, but only according to very specific rules. The transformations all obey *Vahhd*. *Vahhd* rules over all of the material world. There is no escaping it.

Vahhd fills me with a great sense of wonder and awe. How do these transformations happen? Why do they always happen in very specific ways? How does that come about? Who or what is making sure that *Vahhd* rules all, exactly as it does?

These questions are important to me, as is my sense of awe. I must make a confession, however. I must admit that science cannot help me answer these questions. Science does not tell me why *Vahhd* is as it is. Science tells me only that rules exist, and helps me to know what the rules are. Sometimes, it may appear that science is more powerful than that, that science can answer the *why* question. It cannot. Science figures out the rules. It cannot tell us how the rules got there or why the rules exist at all.

In this modern world, many believe that science and logic are the paths towards truth. Yet, science is limited in what it can reveal to us. There is another limitation that you may be less aware of: logic itself is limited. Logic is not a path towards truth. In this modern world, many have proclaimed that scientific truth is superior to religious truth. Yet, the limitations of science and logic teach us that *it is the very nature of this world that certain truths cannot be revealed by science or logic*. These truths that science cannot reveal are important truths that cannot be ignored. We must turn elsewhere than science to reach a deeper understanding of this world.

Limitations to Logic

Logic is very powerful, but logic is also limited. An argument can be completely logical, but utterly wrong. Logical arguments must start with assumptions or premises, which are the starting point in a logical chain of reasoning. An argument that starts with assumptions that are correct, and that uses correct logic, will reach the correct conclusions. Logical arguments can be wrong, not because the logic itself is wrong, but because the starting assumptions are wrong. It is important to realize that very sophisticated arguments can be dead wrong. That happens because these arguments start from incorrect assumptions (also called premises).

Logic alone will not take us towards truth. Logic is a tool that may help us to find truth. (Such is certainly the case for scientific truth: logic plays a central role.) Like any tool, logic can be misused and can lead us astray. It is important to realize that endeavors that are strongly based on logic, endeavors such as science, are not always about truth.

The logic example that I used earlier about movies is a very simple application of logic. The simplicity of it is part of the point I am trying to make: logic is a form of 'common sense' that everyone understands. Even so, seemingly simple and 'obvious' logic is actually not so simple. We have already shown that logic is not sufficient to take us towards truth. Next we discuss why seemingly simple ideas can lead to logical contradictions that lead nowhere. Logic is not as powerful as you might think.

Russell's Paradox

Russell's Paradox is a famous paradox of logic that Bertrand Russell discovered in 1901. Russell was a mathematician and philosopher who is famous for writing a book called *Principia Mathematica* (Principles of Mathematics). In this book, he tried to create a rigorous logical basis for common mathematical ideas such as a 'number'. You can do math without reading or understanding the *Principia*. Yet, Russell wanted to make sure there existed a firm logical basis for mathematics, based on very simple premises that everyone could agree on. Unfortunately, it did not work out as well as he intended.

One of the very simple notions that Russell wanted to work with is the idea of a 'set'. A set is a collection of things or objects. For example, you could have the set consisting of all chairs, or the set consisting of all red chairs. You could have the set of all animals, or the set of all people. It's easy to tell if a particular object is a member of a set, based on how we've defined the collection. Is a dog a member of the set of animals? Of course! Is a pencil a member of the set of all animals? No way! Is a person a member of the set of all people? Yes. What about a person and the set of all animals? Maybe, because it depends on whether you believe that people are animals. That's not a problem. An object can certainly be a member of two sets at once, or even more!

This is simple, right? Wouldn't it be great if we could prove that the concept of 'number' is related to a simple idea such as a set? Sets are so simple, so 'common sense', that they must also be logical (or so Russell thought). If I can base mathematics on the concept of 'set', I'd have a firm logical basis for doing mathematics with numbers. I want to work with numbers to do science and many other things, so I'd like to feel completely sure that the number concept is logical. Not everything in this world needs to be logical, but we expect math and science to be something that is.

What could possibly go wrong with the simple idea of a set? Russell in fact found something terribly wrong. He proved that the simple idea of a set leads to a logical contradiction. *Let's repeat that:* the simple idea of a collection of objects is *logically unsound*. We don't notice the problem because the usual sets and objects that we think about are just fine. However, Russell started to think about some unusual sets and found that the very idea of a set can lead to problems. Let's work out what Russell found. What follows is a rather detailed discussion of sets. Don't worry if you do not follow all the details. It's the conclusion that interests us most.

Russell's new thinking was to consider sets that are members of themselves. At first glance, this is doable. Before we explain that further, let's consider a simpler set: the set of shapes that are circles. If you show me a shape, I can tell if it's a circle or not. If it is, it's in the set. If the shape you show me is not a circle, it's not in the set of circles. Most objects are *not* in the set of all circles.

Russell began to think about particular objects that are not in the set of all circles. In particular, Russell began to think about sets as objects. Why not? A set is a mathematical construct, but it certainly is something we can refer to. So Russell began to think about *a set of sets*, that is, a collection of objects that are sets. The sets themselves are viewed as objects. This is sounding more abstract and mathematical, but not inherently illogical (yet).

Let's focus on some specific examples. What about the *set of all circles*? Is the set of all circles a member of the 'set of all sets'? Yes, by definition it is. Is a circle also a member of the 'set of all sets'? No. A circle is a shape and not a set. But the set of all circles is a set, and therefore the 'set of all circles' belongs to the 'set of all sets'.

Russell started to think more deeply about this 'set of sets' idea. For example, you could think about the set of 'sets containing shapes'. The 'set of all circles' is certainly a set that contains shapes. Therefore, the set of all circles would belong to the set that contained shape sets. Also belonging to the 'set of shape sets' is the 'set of all squares' and the 'set of all rectangles', etc. Perhaps you are not sure where this argument is headed. Bear with me. You must accept the idea that sets themselves are objects that can be collected into a set.

Now things get interesting. We've gone so far as to suggest that I can refer to sets as objects and make new sets from them. Russell in particular began to think about a very strange sort of set, but a set that seems quite logical at first thought. Russell began to think about sets that contain themselves as a member. What could that mean? Let's use some examples. The set of all circles is a set that contains a particular shape. Since a shape is not a set, the set of all circles is not a member of itself. All you find in the set of all circles is circles, not sets. The set of all circles is an example of a set that Russell called 'normal'. A set is 'normal' if that set does *not* contain itself as a member. The 'set of all circles' is normal, according to Russell. That set contains shapes. It does *not* contain any sets.

'Normal' sets are what we usually think about when we think about collections of things.

Russell, being an abstract mathematician, wanted to push this idea further and consider sets that *do* contain themselves as a member. One example would be the 'set of all sets'. Since the 'set of all sets' is a set, the 'set of all sets' contains *itself* as a member. Another example is the set of all things that are not shapes. A set is not a shape, therefore the 'set of things that are not shapes' *is* a member of itself. Russell described such sets – those that belong to themselves – as 'abnormal'. Abnormal sets seem perfectly fine as sets. They are just a little stranger than the 'normal' sets.

Reality check: if all this talk about sets is getting too abstract, don't worry. A simpler version of the Russell Paradox is included below, so skip ahead if you like.

Now we jump to the next level of abstraction. Consider the set of all normal sets. What does this mean? It's a collection of sets that have the 'normal' property (as we defined above). In other words, the set of all normal sets is a collection of sets that do not contain themselves as a member.

Russell then asked a simple question: is the 'set of all normal sets' itself normal? In other words, the question is: does the 'set of all normal sets' contain itself as a member? If the set of all normal sets is normal, that set does not contain itself as a member (normal sets don't hold themselves as members). That leads us to the statement that 'the set of all normal sets' does *not* contain a particular normal set (itself). Then it can't be the set of *all* normal sets, can it? The set of *all* normal sets must contain itself if it is normal. So, we are led to believe that the set of all normal sets is not normal. The answer to Russell's question seems to be simple: the 'set of all normal sets' is in fact not a normal set itself.

But wait! If the set of all normal sets is not normal, then the set of normal sets is a member of itself. Logic demands that we conclude this. Recall that sets that are *not* normal contain themselves as members. The set of all normal sets is *not* normal, meaning it *is* a member of itself. So, by strictly logical arguments about simple ideas such as 'collections' or 'sets', we've reached a logically absurd result. There exists a set that is not normal only if it is normal. Ouch! Not good from a logical perspective.

The logical paradox is basically this: there exists at least one set that is a member of itself and not a member of itself at the same time. If you try to base mathematics on that sort of paradoxical logic, you'll get really strange math, such as 1 = 2. The concept of a number is not very useful if 1 = 2. Something is not right.

What Russell and others concluded is that even simple ideas of a 'set' and ideas of logic can lead to contradictory results. More restricted ideas of a set were then developed that circumvented the difficulties. Nevertheless, mathematicians and philosophers learned a sobering lesson: simple ideas combined with logic have their limits. What may appear as very simple and logical can actually be a quagmire. If we're lucky, we'll catch the limitations and not develop our science based on contradictory ideas. If we're not lucky, we'll realize we're wrong only after lots of work has been done going down the wrong path.

Russell's Paradox: Simpler Version

A simpler version of the Russell Paradox is known as the Barber Paradox. Russell himself used it to illustrate his ideas. The Barber Paradox starts with some very simple-sounding premises. Imagine a town with just one professional barber, who is a man. Every man in this town shaves. Townspeople either shave themselves or use the barber. The barber has adopted the following reasonable policy: he only shaves those men who don't shave themselves.

The above scenario certainly appears reasonable. In fact, we'll find out that the scenario is impossible. Let's ask a simple question: 'Does the barber shave himself?' If he does, then the barber is violating his policy that he only shaves those who do *not* shave themselves. If the barber does *not* shave himself, then we need to invoke the rule that the barber shaves all who do not shave themselves. Invoking this rule, we find that the barber does shave himself. So, according to the rules, if the barber does not shave himself, he does shave himself. Similarly, if the barber does not shave himself, he does shave himself. And so, a paradox.

What this paradox teaches us is that we can state some simple ideas that appear clear and logical, which are in fact contradictory and absurd. Unfortunately, we do not know immediately if the simple ideas lead to logical contradictions. We need to ask the right questions and think about consequences. If we're smart enough and a little lucky, we *might* realize that the ideas lead to nonsense. Who knows what other ideas that we hold dear are, in fact, impossible? The situation in the town as we've stated it is logically flawed and cannot actually exist. The barber's policy cannot be enforced. We only realized the absurdity of the situation after we asked a simple but profound question: who shaves the barber? What if we had not asked the question? We might never have realized that the ideas we formed were not possible.

Even simple logic, which is a form of 'common sense' that everyone understands, can create conceptual difficulties. All this goes to show that logic and seemingly 'obvious' ideas are not a guaranteed path towards 'absolute truth'. Simple intuitive ideas and logic can sometimes lead to absurd and contradictory results. The path towards 'absolute truth' must lie elsewhere.

Back to *Vahhd*

We have said that *Vahhd* strictly follows logical rules, everywhere and always. All scientists believe that, implicitly or explicitly. We have also learned that logic has its limits. We can create logically contradictory situations starting with very simple ideas or assumptions. We may not know of the contradictions unless we ask specific questions that 'rat out' the system and reveal it for what it is.

Not all logical constructions are contradictory. Scientists believe that the logical construction that governs how nature behaves is not a contradictory one. *Vahhd* is not absurd but beautiful, or so scientists believe. Any physics text you find will teach that the logical rules governing nature are not contradictory. Scientists cannot imagine a world where the rules that govern nature contain a logical contradiction. When scientists find such examples, they assume they've got the rules wrong.

The scientific belief in the 'consistency' of nature's logic led to Einstein's theory of relativity. Einstein proposed a simple and beautifully logical way to reconcile experiments that searched for an 'ether' in which light traveled. As it turns out, the ether does not exist, although scientists before Einstein assumed it had to. The search for the ether was very reasonable and logical. It seemed to be needed to make the laws governing nature logically consistent. Einstein was the first to realize the ether was not needed. A different set of natural laws could explain the experiments without the need for an ether. That new set of natural laws became the principles of Relativity Theory. Logical conflicts were avoided. Einstein did not change *Vahhd*, but he did change our understanding of *Vahhd*.

We now turn our attention to science, which is a way to learn about the 'logically correct' rules that govern nature. *Vahhd* is all-important in our lives. Let's see how science and *Vahhd* work together.

3

Science

Science is a way to learn about *Vahhd*. The scientific method of discovery and learning is a search for the logical rules that nature follows. In this chapter, we describe how science is done, what it is, and what it is not. What you learn may surprise you. Science and the technological advances that arise from new scientific knowledge have transformed our world. To continue on our spiritual journey, we must have a deep understanding of what science is.

Science has taught us much about the natural world in the last few hundred years. As science has advanced, so have the instruments that science uses, such as telescopes, to teach us more and more. It's been a wonderfully successful enterprise. At this moment in the development of science, scientists have developed a story of 'creation', of the first few minutes of the universe that they believe came into being about 14 billion years ago. I will describe that creation story later in this chapter. I call this story the 'Scientific Genesis' story, or SciGen for short.

The story of SciGen is fundamental to much of what we discuss in this book. Your belief or lack of belief in SciGen is an important marker for your journey. You must know SciGen to continue on the journey.

Scientific Revolutions
In the preceding paragraphs, I referred to 'this moment' in the development of science. I can explain why I used that phrase. The body of scientific knowledge is always changing. The essence of scientific discovery is to change what we know. The scientific facts that we believe today may change sometime in the

future. Scientific facts are not immutable or permanent, but based on the available evidence at hand. As new evidence comes in, we often change our version of scientific facts to fit the evidence. What we 'know' today about the creation of the universe is not necessarily what we will 'know' or believe in the future.

You may be thinking: new scientific facts build upon previous knowledge, so as discoveries are made we simply add to our knowledge but do not change what we've known in the past. Although that can be true, often it is not. Often, new scientific results don't just add to what we know, but fundamentally change what we know (or what we thought we knew). What we used to believe true becomes false, and new knowledge takes its place. Science often advances by replacing past knowledge with new knowledge, not simply by adding to existing knowledge. The reason that old knowledge is replaced has to do with the fact that nature follows logical rules (as we talked about earlier). The logic of nature has to be consistent and 'hang together'. A single new scientific fact can show that the entire existing logical structure is incorrect. To create the correct new understanding, the old structure has to be dismantled and a new one created in its stead. One cannot simply add to the existing knowledge if the new knowledge logically contradicts what had been known before.

Scientific facts are interconnected in a complex web of logic. Even one or two new facts can change our understanding of a large number of previously held beliefs. A 'scientific revolution' happens when a large number of scientific facts change all at once due to new knowledge. Such 'revolutions' have happened numerous times in the past and will continue in the future. Two examples are: Einstein's theory of relativity, and the birth of quantum mechanics. Both of these scientific revolutions happened in the first part of the 20th century.

We summarize this aspect of science by saying that scientific knowledge is *provisional*. Scientific facts are based on an ever-changing body of evidence. If I do a new experiment, or reinterpret an old one, the body of evidence can change. As the evidence changes, so might existing scientific 'facts'. This may surprise you. Isn't a 'fact' a 'fact'? How can doing a new experiment change an existing fact? It can, because science is more than just a collection of experiments. Science uses concepts and ideas to *interpret* the measurements. In other words, we could write this 'equation':

Scientific knowledge = experiments + concepts

Science is about what we measure (experiments) *and* about ideas we use to interpret the measurements. You cannot have the science without the interpretation.

I want to be very clear on this point: a new experiment cannot alter the results of previous experiments. Experimental results are a form of evidence, and evidence is what it is. Rather, new experiments can radically change existing scientific facts because new experiments change our conceptual understanding of past experimental results.

This point is very important, about what scientific knowledge really is. In the next section, I will explain that the *scientific method* is why scientific knowledge has a provisional character. Before I do that, I want to point out something important. Scientific knowledge consists of experiments and concepts. Experiments are something we can measure, sense and touch. Experimental results are tangible and material. *Concepts are not.* Concepts cannot be seen, touched or smelled. They live somewhere outside our material world. It's important to realize that scientific knowledge is a combination of the seen and unseen. We will return to this point later on in this book. If all you trust is what you see (or touch or smell), then you do not trust science. Science goes beyond the seeable. Why this is so is discussed next.

The Scientific Method

At its core, science is about a 'method' or 'process' we call the *scien-*

tific method. The scientific method has been used for hundreds of years and has led to an explosion of new knowledge and an explosion of practical benefits built upon that knowledge. A deeper understanding of the scientific method will allow us to understand what scientific knowledge is, and what it is not. In this chapter, we will learn how science evolves to explain an ever-increasing set of experiments, and how one or a few new experiments can radically change past scientific knowledge. We will learn how the scientific process does not reveal 'Absolute Truth'. The kind of truth that science provides is *provisional* truth, truth that may change in the future. Scientific truth, by its very nature, is transitory and ever-changing. It is not and cannot be 'Absolute'. If you seek 'Absolute Truth', you cannot rely on science to provide it for you. The 'Absolute Truth' we discussed in the previous chapter is not a part of the scientific method. Absolute Truth is still truth, but it is not a scientific truth.

Scientific knowledge is gained by applying the scientific method. The scientific method is a way to create new scientific knowledge using experiments. Experiments are based on measuring properties of the material world. You can think of experiments as sophisticated and advanced sense organs, such as eyes and ears. In the past, mankind only had eyes and ears to do scientific experiments, and these sensory organs are still needed today. Of course, scientific instruments have gone much beyond our naked eyes and ears, just as a telescope allows us to see things in the heavens that we could not see with our unaided eyes. There is no fundamental difference between a naked eye and an eye looking through a telescope. Both can form the basis for scientific experiments that we use to build scientific knowledge.

Understanding the method tells us something about the knowledge we have gained. The major conceptual breakthrough that the scientific method provided when it was developed in the 1500s is that science pays close attention to experiments. Before the scientific method, there were philosophers who engaged in 'meta-physical' reasoning about the material world around us. These philosophers sought to learn about the material world just as scientists do today, but they did not think it was very important to do careful experiments. They tried to learn about the material world by thinking, using logical arguments and imagination. They did use their observations about the material world to guide them, but they did not bother to do carefully controlled experiments. Compared to what scientists accomplish today, these 'natural philosophers' achieved very little in the way of practical benefits.

The breakthrough that resulted in the scientific method is simple to describe, but profound in its consequences: the scientific method involves the crucial idea of a *test*. The meta-physical philosophers would observe things and develop ideas about how nature worked, but they would not bother to test those ideas using experiments. Scientists, on the other hand, are not so free to believe what they want. Scientists form ideas about how nature works, about the logical rules that govern nature, about *Vahhd*, but they do not accept an idea until it is *tested*. A test can support a new scientific idea, or it can suggest the idea is wrong. If the test, using experiments, supports the idea then new scientific knowledge is being gained. But remember: this new knowledge is provisional. New experiments, or even new ideas about the same experiments, can lead to a rejection or wholesale changing of this new knowledge.

The scientific method binds scientific knowledge closely to the logical structure of the material world. Scientific ideas and concepts are bound closely to *Vahhd*. Our scientific knowledge, as successful though imperfect as it is, as impermanent and transitory as it is, is intimately connected to *Vahhd*. They are not apart from each other. Scientific knowledge reflects or describes, however imperfectly, the logical structure of nature. If you believe that the material world is God's creation, then science can help bring you a greater understanding of God's creation. For this reason alone, you will benefit from an interest in science.

The pre-scientific natural philosophers were not so connected to *Vahhd*. Although they did observe the world to some degree, they were bound to it loosely. Their ideas and concepts often took precedence over experiment. We can therefore view science as a progression towards humility: whereas the natural philosophers trusted their own thoughts and minds to a large extent, scientists are forced to submit their ideas to a test. Ideas about how nature works must be carefully tested, and those ideas changed if the experiments suggest it. In science, experiment trumps ideas, rather than the other way around.

For believers, there is another path to Truth: the holy word (*'Thy word is truth'*). For those who believe in the Bible or take it literally, a conflict can arise between scientific truth and the revealed word of God. This conflict need not arise in all matters of the spirit, as we will discover later. The conflict arises when the holy word describes natural events or natural histories. From what we know of the scientific method and scientific truth, it may appear that the conflict between the word and scientific truth is a conflict with logic itself. Scientific truth is about discovering the logical rules that nature obeys. If the word contradicts scientific truth, it shakes the very foundations of logic, because scientists believe that nature follows logical rules *all the time*. Let's focus on this apparent conflict in a little more detail. We will find that the conflict is not so absolute as it first appears.

Scientific truths are the result of logical reasoning about a material world that is, according to science, utterly logical. If a revealed truth contradicts a scientific fact, does that revelation contradict logic itself? Let's consider a miraculous occurrence, such as turning water into wine. Scientific truth forbids that Jesus performed this miracle at a wedding. Yet, since scientific truth is *provisional*, a scientist cannot claim with absolute certainty that the miraculous event did not occur. Certainly, no scientist alive today has any idea how such a miracle could occur, by the laws of nature we know now. At the same time, a scientist cannot claim with absolute certainty that the miracle did not occur. Therefore, a contradiction between scientific and revealed truth is not the same as rejecting logic or 'common sense'.

Logic need not be suspect when scientific truth is apparently violated by miracles. What may be happening is that our understanding of the material world is incomplete. Turning water into wine does not necessarily contradict *Vahhd*. The contradiction may appear only because we don't have a full grasp of the rules that govern the material world. Violating logic is a very hard thing for humans to do. We are at root so tied to it.

The belief that 'the material world behaves differently from how we expect' is consistent with miracles and consistent with science itself. 'Different from what we expect' is what scientific revolutions are all about. If your faith leads you to believe that Jesus performed miracles, then the easiest way to explain that is to suggest that the natural laws as we understand them now are incomplete. That is an explanation that is consistent with the miracle, consistent with logic, and consistent with scientific truth and the 'Absolute Truth' that we discussed in Chapter 2.

Let's consider the belief that the earth is about 4,000 years old. This belief does not come from science, but from a literal reading of the Bible. Scientists believe the earth is far older than 4,000 years (about 4 billion years older, to be more exact). The scientific view is not based on a competing religious belief in the traditional sense. Scientists believe this age based on their application of the *scientific method*. An example of this method is presented next in the form of a story that could apply to any of us. Jeremy is a man who believes literally in the Bible and this is his story:

When I was a boy, I planted two trees in the back part of my yard. Ten years later, I felled one of them. I noticed that inside the tree trunk there were rings, and I noticed there was one ring for each year the tree was alive. This caused me to guess that when a tree grows, a new ring is formed every year. I decided to test my guess when, five years later, it was time to chop down the second tree. Lo and behold, the older tree had five more rings, one for each year that passed. I became more confident that my guess was correct: a growing tree adds one ring per year.

Sometime after this second tree was chopped down, I received a phone call from an old friend of mine who wanted to go camping with me in an old wood in Northern California. I had heard that trees there were thousands of years old. This got me to thinking: would there be thousands of rings in the trunk of such an old tree? Wouldn't it be cool if my idea about tree rings were true also for trees much older than mine and located elsewhere?

Luckily, there happened to be a felled tree in that forest with the large and ancient trees. I was able to clearly see the inside of the trunk and I started to count the rings that were clearly visible also. I counted over 4,500 rings! That tree was really old. Then I was struck by a very depressing fact: the tree is older than the earth itself! This set me to doubting my own mind and vexed me for a long time.

Jeremy is understandably upset. He seems to have come across two *contradictory* truths. One truth, revealed to him by the Bible, is that the earth is about 4,000 years old. The second 'truth', revealed to him by the scientific method, is that the tree, and therefore the earth, is older than 4,500 years. Being a human being of sound mind, it is not surprising that Jeremy was upset, because the contradiction of these two truths violated his deep-seated acceptance of *logic*. Logic does not permit these two contradictory truths. Being human, Jeremy knew and swore by logic. He also had faith. He could not reconcile logic with faith.

Jeremy (and others like him!) should understand that there is a way out of this dilemma. You can believe in both your faith and in logic if you realize that your knowledge of nature's rules is incomplete. Not fully knowing the rules of nature is acceptable to faith and also to science. In the story as I've described it above, it *seems* as if the contradiction is inescapable. Jeremy certainly did apply the scientific method to his observations, and the scientific method is certainly a method based on logic. The contradiction is avoided because *logic alone is not a path towards truth*. Logic is a way of transforming one set of truths into another set of truths. Logic supplies rules for these transformations. However, logic does not supply a starting point, an initial set of truths (premises), from which you can then apply logic.

Let's examine Jeremy's situation more closely. He certainly made a good guess about trees adding one ring to their trunks every year. He confirmed that guess with an experiment in his own backyard. His eventual dismay was based on yet another guess: that the trees in a faraway Northern California forest obeyed the same rules as the trees in his backyard. Most of us would agree that's a pretty solid guess: trees are trees, whether they are in our backyards or in a faraway land. At root, however, we need to realize that it is a guess. Stating that trees in Northern California follow the same rules as trees in our backyard is a *guess* or *assumption*; it is *not* a logical deduction. Jeremy could have saved himself a great deal of vexation if he was more aware of when he was applying logic, and when he was just guessing. If Jeremy had considered that 'trees are not all the same', he could have maintained his strong biblical faith and his belief in logic. Let's create a new ending to Jeremy's story:

> ...Then I was struck by a depressing fact: the tree is older than the earth itself! I immediately realized I had made a mistake. I had incorrectly assumed that the trees in this wondrous forest were similar to the trees in my small backyard. Clearly, these majestic trees are different! For if they were not, the earth could not be 4,500 years old, the age I have learned in my biblical studies. I did not have a clue as to why or how these trees were

different, but I knew they must be, so I set out to figure out why.

This story now has a happier ending! Jeremy maintains both his faith and his ability to use logic. The reason is that he questioned his guess or *assumption* about the similarity of all trees. Assuming that Northern California trees are the same as those in his backyard really is a guess.

I want to make my message here clear. I am not trying to suggest that there really is a large difference between trees in the forest and trees in Jeremy's backyard. I am trying to make the point that, although science is a logical discipline and nature itself behaves logically, science is not completely based on logic. You cannot use logic alone to reach scientific truth. You have to make assumptions also.

An 'assumption' is something that you believe to be true even if you don't have proof. In many ways, an assumption is similar to a guess. We all make lots of assumptions in our lives, every day. We have to, because we don't have the time to test everything that we believe is true. The role of and the need for assumptions within the scientific method is actually more fundamental than a lack of time. Assumptions are needed to test hypotheses and interpret experiments. Assumptions, by their very nature, could turn out to be wrong. And so it is with science: when assumptions do turn out to be wrong it leads to 'scientific revolutions' that radically change how scientists view the world and interpret experiments.

We see that Jeremy was acting like a scientist when he made assumptions about how trees grow rings. Scientists make those kinds of assumptions all the time. In fact, scientists do believe that all trees are very similar and that they grow one ring per year. That is one reason why scientists believe the earth is older than 4,500 years. There are many, many additional reasons why scientists believe the earth is 4 billion+ years old. Fundamentally, those reasons are based on the scientific method. As we've seen, the scientific method is based on a combination of logic and assumptions.

It's not all logic, so believing something that scientists don't believe does not mean you are violating the rules of logic. It usually means you are working with assumptions that are different from those of a scientist.

Jeremy's story is an example of how scientific truth can contradict truth that is revealed from a holy book. Such contradictions are not about logical inconsistency, but about assumptions. While we're on the subject of assumptions, it's worth considering how scientists choose their assumptions. A detailed look at this would take us too far into other matters, but there is an aspect of scientific assumptions you should be aware of. Scientific assumptions are based on 'educated guesses'. In fact, new scientific knowledge is gained based on guessing. Scientific knowledge accumulates when scientists guess what the logical rules of nature are. We know of no way to discover those rules except by guessing. Jeremy uses a scientifically accepted way to determine age using tree rings. Scientists believe that counting tree rings is a reliable way to determine the age of a tree for many, many types of trees. Scientists believe this because many experiments have supported this idea.

Guesses are needed at the early stages of a new scientific discovery. It may surprise some of you that a fundamental act required to increase scientific knowledge is nothing more than a guess. If you are surprised, then you are probably underestimating the importance and value of guesswork. There is no other way to acquire new scientific knowledge than by guessing. Religious truth is 'revealed' from a holy source, such as the Bible. Scientific truth starts with a guess. We can see this by returning to our description of the scientific method. Scientists must formulate a hypothesis about how nature behaves before they can devise a test to confirm or reject the hypothesis. The act of 'forming a hypothesis' is nothing more than coming up with a guess. There is no other way. If you thought that scientific hypotheses are always the result of logical deduction, you would not be correct. Richard P. Feynman, the eminent 20th-century physicist, writes in his books about the importance of guessing. The most important scientific advances, the ones that really shake things up, are almost always the result of a really good guess.

Feynman had special 'tricks of the trade' he would use to come up with good guesses. Feynman won the Nobel Prize in physics for work he did in a field called 'quantum electrodynamics', which is a scientific theory about the electric and magnetic forces. A fellow physicist named Julian Schwinger shared the Nobel Prize for the same theory. It may have been Schwinger who had the first correct guesses about how these forces work, along with another scientist who shared the prize: Sin-Itiro Tomonaga. Feynman provided another conceptual understanding of the same basic theory, but that made it much easier to do calculations to test the theory. Schwinger was widely celebrated for his scientific brilliance, which means he had an uncanny ability to guess right. The same was true of Feynman. Guessing the rules of nature is very, very difficult, and only a few brilliant minds can do it really well. Nobody really knows how these geniuses learned to be so good at guessing. It's not a talent that is easily taught in schools. (Have you ever taken a class in 'how to guess'?)

There are many examples of brilliant guesswork in the recent history of science. Albert Einstein's most famous guess led to his theory of relativity and thus to the famous equation $E = mc^2$, which eventually led to the development of the atomic bomb. Einstein made a guess about the results of a famous experiment that had been performed in the late 1800s. That experiment was designed to measure properties of the mysterious 'ether', a wondrous fluid that surrounds the earth and helps electric and magnetic waves (including light) propagate through space. Einstein's guess, which led to his famous relativity theory, is that the ether did not in fact exist. Einstein believed scientists were on a wild goose chase when they searched for the ether. Einstein's new theory was a way to explain a famous experiment (the 'Michelson-Morley' experiment) without the need for an ether.

Later in his life, Einstein made guesses about atoms and subatomic particles that turned out to be wrong. Einstein is regarded as a father of the modern quantum theory, the scientific theory that describes atoms and subatomic particles. Yet, the quantum theory developed in a way he did not like. Einstein's guesses about quantum theory were different from those of another brilliant young physicist named Werner Heisenberg. Following years of futility in which scientists thrashed about trying to guess how atoms worked, Heisenberg tried a radical idea and got it right. The process of scientific discovery is far from strictly logical and straightforward. If you want to be a great scientist, it may be far more productive to hone your skills of intuition rather than logic, although both are needed to succeed.

I hope this discussion of the scientific method has increased your understanding. It's important for where we want to go next: the scientific view of how the universe began. I call this the 'scientific story of Genesis', because I want to contrast it with the biblical story of Genesis. It turns out that scientists have developed their own 'creation story' of how the universe began.

The 'Scientific Genesis' Story

We are now ready for the 'scientific story of Genesis'. Genesis means 'the origin or coming into being of something'. The scientific story of Genesis is how scientists view the beginning of the universe. It is the scientists' view of the beginning of the world. That view, which I will call SciGen, is based on the scientific method and is widely accepted by scientists today. As with any scientific theory, it is *provisional*, meaning it is our best understanding based on the facts as we know them today. Who knows how this story will change in the future?

SciGen is an important part of the scientist's 'worldview'. SciGen is based on the laws of nature and how the material world changes over vast stretches of time – billions of years. SciGen does not invoke a creator in the traditional religious sense. There is no need in SciGen for a Supreme God-like Being to act on the material world. All that is needed for SciGen are the laws of nature. Perhaps SciGen violates your religious beliefs. However, one can believe in SciGen and a divine creator at the same time. SciGen does not need to invoke a creator and does not refer to one. SciGen also does not rule out the creator's existence.

SciGen is central to this book because this book is about how science and scientific truth can lead to gifts of the spirit. The path from science to spirituality is fundamentally based on SciGen. Later in this book we will describe how SciGen can lead to a greater spiritual understanding. These spiritual gifts are available to you now *with your active participation.*

We now describe:

SciGen: The Scientific Story of Genesis

In the beginning was the law. The law ruled over all matter and energy in the universe.

In the beginning, the universe was very hot and dense. Energy and matter reverberated within it, without form.

Thereby did it come to pass that the universe began to expand. In this expansion, the energy and matter began to cool, and matter began to adopt form from the formless expanse.

And this matter did spread throughout the universe. As the universe grew, the matter would form clumps, and the clumps would combine into larger pieces, and lo, stars and planets did form.

The planets cooled and some of these became wet and filled with water. Upon the planet's surface, molecules did appear that became alive. And life did thrive and did multiply and over the eons the life became beasts of this world.

And the beasts did thrive and multiply over the eons and there came to be beasts who were like man, who were not yet man.

More eons passed and like-man begat man, as the natural law acted and was steady. And man did awake and become aware and became the ruler of this earth. As man ruled, so did he develop a hunger for the spirit and for worship, and a hunger for truth that is not of this world.

That is the story of creation, as it is known this Anno Domini 2011.

Our version of SciGen is brief but it has the elements we need to guide us in our journey. There are several striking aspects of SciGen:

1) 'Creation moment': scientists now believe that the universe began with a 'bang' (the scientific term is the 'Big Bang'). Such a belief was not always the scientific consensus. Many scientists used to believe in a 'steady state' universe that was more or less the same throughout all time. That was a reasonable idea before evidence accumulated from newer, bigger and better telescopes. The only way that scientists could explain the new evidence was to suggest the universe had a 'creation moment'. The universe was not in a steady state as thought earlier.

2) Humanity is an accident: the wondrous thing we call life and humanity came about by accident. There is no hint in SciGen that human life had to happen, or that the universe is constructed so that it will happen. SciGen simply documents the fact that humanity happened, and places no particular value on life and humanity, either positive or negative.

3) The laws of nature are ever-present and eternal: the existence of natural law governing all the material world is an ever-present reality in SciGen. However, the forms that exist in the universe, the material world itself, are transitory and ever-changing. The logical rules of *Vahhd* are ever-present and eternal. The forms that *Vahhd* rules over are

transitory, as dust that blows in the wind.

Now it is time to understand the implications of SciGen. If SciGen is true, how does that help me? What spiritual truths can I learn from SciGen?

Let's step back and think about the implications of SciGen. For example, nature is eternally governed by natural law, and *Vahhd* rules all the material universe. SciGen gives no hint as to why. To ask why is to go beyond science. Science and SciGen provide no answers to these questions.

Where does human value come from in SciGen? In SciGen, life and humanity are simply complex forms of matter with no special status. SciGen has nothing to say about the value of humanity, unlike the biblical Genesis story. SciGen also does not contain any notion of right and wrong. SciGen is a story of the material world, and human beings are merely complex forms of matter within the material world. SciGen by itself cannot help us to understand right and wrong or to find our sense of values. SciGen does not tell us what to believe in.

Yet, SciGen can help us in our journey. When I ponder SciGen, I am awestruck by the majesty and scale of this story. The universe is so vast and complex, and startlingly beautiful. The material universe is full of wondrous events, all governed by and determined by a set of natural laws that are all-encompassing and ever-present. Yet, the material universe does not seem to speak directly to me. The master of this universe, *Vahhd*, does not acknowledge my existence. Natural law goes on and on, forever and ever, without regard for me. Am I therefore insignificant?

The lesson of SciGen is the challenge it contains for us. The challenge posed by SciGen is this: there is a vast universe outside us, with forces eternal and omnipresent beyond our full understanding. SciGen challenges us to find meaning in this universe. As awe-inspiring as SciGen is, it contains a huge void. SciGen cannot fill the void of meaning. That is the great challenge facing humanity: to believe in meaning.

Our great challenge is to create meaning and have it co-exist with the all-powerful *Vahhd*. Yes, *Vahhd* is all-powerful but its domain is limited to the material universe. *Vahhd* is all-powerful only within its domain. I do not challenge *Vahhd* in its domain, for I know *Vahhd* rules all, forever and without fear.

Yet *Vahhd* cannot satisfy my hunger for meaning, for values, for belief in right and wrong. *I am significant! My life does have meaning! Every day matters! My family is important to me!* Yet, *Vahhd* will not show this to me directly. *Vahhd* merely challenges me to find it. *Vahhd's* power is truly great, but it can neither help nor hinder my belief in meaning.

I believe that humanity is worth cherishing. *Vahhd* challenges me to put this belief on the same great stage as the material universe. And so I declare: *Vahhd, your power is great. Yet, equally great is my belief that human life and humankind are of value.* On our journey forward, life's meaning and natural law shall walk together as equals.

SciGen is the springboard from which we must find our way. SciGen is the launching point for our spiritual journey. Our journey is a child of SciGen and derives from it. So we must understand SciGen, to better understand the journey.

The next idea that we will discuss is a concept known as 'simulation'. It is an important idea within SciGen, so I will describe it very carefully in the next section. Simulation presents another great challenge in our quest for spiritual enlightenment.

SciGen and Simulation: Science at the Extremes

Consider that SciGen may not be a modern idea. Perhaps SciGen was guessed at in ancient times. There may have been a great spiritual leader thousands of years ago who pondered this idea: what if mankind is no different from the dust that blows in the wind? What if mankind is but a version of dust, coming from the dust and returning to dust? For so it is written: *Ashes to ashes, dust to dust.*

The spiritual leader would have been aware of the challenge posed by such an idea: that we are no different from dust. Thousands of years ago, the story of SciGen could not have been known, since the tools of modern science did not yet exist. Yet, there may have been a notion that something like natural law existed, and perhaps mankind is governed by it. That poses a great challenge to our belief in meaning. We do not believe that a speck of dust is alive, or has a sense of meaning. If we are simply material things, as are specks of dust, then how do we find meaning in our own lives?

In this chapter, I wish to explore this question using an idea derived from SciGen. This idea is embedded within the very concept of SciGen, and poses a great challenge to our belief in meaning. The idea is called 'simulation'. Simulation is the act of calculating how nature behaves. In these modern times, such calculations are done using computers. Using simulation, scientists can answer questions about how a parachute will open, or how a cannonball flies through the air, even if they don't have those objects physically next to them. Simulations are not perfect, but they are very useful and can reveal a great deal of information about the world around us. Our interest in simulation is this: if human beings are nothing more than material objects, can human beings be simulated? What challenge does that pose to our belief in meaning?

The fundamental idea behind simulation is simple: it is that natural law is fundamentally based on the rules of logic. Computing machines can simulate logical reasoning. Using simulation to predict how nature behaves is a way of recreating how natural law imposes logical transformations onto the material world. In the 'real world', natural law and the rules of logic transform nature from one moment to the next. A simulation imitates this transformation process, thereby predicting how nature behaves. The connection between simulation, logic, and natural law are very close.

We can imagine building a computing machine powerful enough to 'out-think' *Vahhd*. Can we produce a machine that, while not as all-powerful as *Vahhd*, can at least peer into *Vahhd*'s 'soul' and learn what *Vahhd* will do? Scientists believe the answer is yes. This poses a huge challenge to our belief in meaning, because the idea of simulation raises a frightening possibility: will simulation reveal that human beings are nothing more than 'computing machines'? SciGen tells us that human beings are nothing more than material objects. Simulation has proven that the behavior of material objects can be calculated by a computer. My mind and thoughts, my hopes and dreams are viewed, within SciGen, as nothing more than a thrashing about of the atoms and molecules within my brain. My brain is itself a material object, ruled by the rules of logic. The behavior of such an object can be simulated. Can I be simulated too? If so, does that mean I am really a kind of computing machine? Do I have more or less value than such a machine? How would I know that? What would a simulated human be like? Would it have a soul?

In SciGen, humans are just another physical (material) system, similar to an atom, a crystal, or the earth's atmosphere and oceans. There is no doubt about the effectiveness of simulation as regards these physical systems. For example, simulation is often used in safety-critical situations such as designing airplane wings. The mathematical equations that describe how air flows around an airplane's wing are solved by (or simulated within) a computer. In many cases, simulation is a valid substitute for real experiments using wind tunnels.

Suppose, then, that we had the technical ability to simulate a human being in a similar way. In reality, there is no way to do that now. Computers just aren't powerful enough and our under-standing of humans is too limited. Computers can't do enough logical transformations fast enough to be useful for simulating a 'system' as complex as a human being. For the sake of argument, let's imagine computers *are* powerful enough, and imagine that we could build a computer program that simulates a human being. What would happen?

A simulated human poses several vexing problems. Would such a human have free will? If the human were simulated on 'standard' computer hardware of the future (much, much faster than what we have today) then it would be possible to obtain detailed information on the entire thought process of a simulated human (or *simhuman*). You could learn the simhuman's thoughts before they happened. With a slightly faster version of simhuman in your back pocket, you could actually know what simhuman was about to think before simhuman thought it himself. Imagine how a simhuman would feel if I revealed to him that I could know all his thoughts and actions before he did, that I could know his 'freely chosen' thoughts and actions before he was aware of them. My guess is that the simhuman would feel, well, less than human and less than free. But according to SciGen, there is no essential difference between a human and a simhuman.

Simulation makes the challenge to meaning posed by SciGen frighteningly real. Although technologically we are very, very far from having the knowledge and computing power to simulate full-up human beings, the idea that it might be doable is haunting us.

The idea of simulation leads us to consider these implications of SciGen:

1) Free will is not real, but an illusion.
2) A human being could be constructed piece by piece out of inanimate matter, perhaps finally proving that human beings are just another form of inanimate matter.
3) The complexities of the human psyche, including our motivations and our soul, are nothing more than complicated 'computations' that could take place just as well on an ordinary computer.

In other words, are human beings nothing more than computing *machines*? Millions of computers are disposed of every year as ordinary trash. Is there nothing fundamentally different about human beings? *Could humans be disposed of in the same way if it served some purpose? Why not?* If we are just 'computing machines', then how do we derive our sense of meaning and value? *We believe we are much more than mere machines, don't we?*

SciGen and the End of Free Will

Let's focus on the idea that SciGen means the end of free will as we know it. This has profound implications beyond just the depressing fact that a machine could out-think me, thought for thought.

Free will is an essential basis for morality. Can a person be moral if they do not have free will? Not by our normal definition of morality. The idea of choosing between right and wrong is central to our concept of morality. One cannot behave morally if one cannot freely choose one's actions. Also, a person cannot be called immoral or evil if they are not choosing to violate what is right. For example, if a person unknowingly and accidentally leaves a store with an item he did not purchase, that person is not doing something immoral. He might be stealing in a strictly defined way, but it is not an immoral act. The person did not choose to do the wrong thing.

Another example is accidentally falling from a building and landing on another person and killing them. No one would call that 'murder', with all the moral overtones that murder entails. The killing is accidental. It is not an immoral act. Such a killing does not mean that the 'killer', the one who fell, is a bad person or has chosen a path towards immorality. The accidental nature of the killing precludes us calling it murder. The killer (loosely speaking) did not choose to harm another person, since the fall is accidental. No intention to kill is involved. Choosing the 'right' path is key to the concept of moral behavior, as is choosing to avoid the 'wrong' path. Without the ability to choose, morality is a non-issue.

Now let's return to SciGen. According to SciGen, human beings are material systems that can be simulated. *Such a system cannot have free will.* The reason is that there is nothing 'free' about the laws of nature that govern the material universe. How the material world behaves is completely predetermined by the logical laws of nature. There is nothing 'free' about *Vahhd*. Simulation proves that. According to SciGen, human beings are not free to make moral choices, despite what may appear. The behavior of material systems can be predicted in advance. Therefore, nothing about human behavior is 'free' in the sense that it is actually chosen. Humans behave according to the laws of nature, and the consequences of those laws can be predicted in advance.

Most people believe they can make choices between right and wrong. How does SciGen explain that? It is explained by saying that free will is an *illusion*. We think we make choices, but we actually don't. The choices are made for us, by the laws of nature. We are simply not aware this is happening. If we could make choices with our free will, we would not be able to always predict what our choices might be. That is what free will is all about. We have a choice to make, we think about it, and then we choose. If someone is able to know in advance the choice that will be made, we don't consider that choice as 'free'. The choice is predetermined, or knowable in advance.

SciGen and the possibility of simulation means that whatever I choose can be known in advance. Suppose a simhuman exists that is a simulation of me. If I speed up the simhuman's computer circuits, I can watch as the simhuman makes all the decisions that I am about to make. The simhuman proves that my decisions are not made freely, because they can all be predicted in advance. Being able to predict a 'free choice' in advance proves that the choosing was not actually 'free'. The idea behind free choice is that we decide what to do. If that decision is pre-ordained, it is not a free decision, and free will is not a part of it.

SciGen Means that Free Will Is an Illusion

SciGen and the destruction of free will present a formidable challenge to our quest for meaning. First, SciGen tells us that there is no essential difference between human beings and any other material thing, such as a car or computer. A human being is made of atoms and molecules, just like everything else. Second, SciGen tells us that what we thought were free decisions are really not free. Our decisions and moral 'choices' are nothing more than the consequence of natural law. Natural law is ever-present and all-encompassing. There is no 'free choice' involved. Natural law is not about deciding, but about predictable behavior. We can predict how natural objects behave, so there is no 'freedom' for things obeying natural law. SciGen says human beings are such things. We are, in effect, not made in God's image but made in the image of natural law. It governs us totally. Free will and moral choice are illusions.

The answer to this great challenge that SciGen poses for us is discussed in Chapter 5. Right now, you should consider the following thought: how can I believe in goodness and in my doing right if I am not really choosing? There is an answer to this question, a way to find meaning in the face of SciGen. The answer has to do with the nature of SciGen itself. We will find a way to meaning. Read on.

4

The Seen and the Unseen

All human life depends on the seen and the unseen. Science depends on the unseen. Fundamentally we all depend on the unmeasurable.

Before moving further along on our journey, we will clarify ideas we have discussed so far. Our book so far has discussed to a great extent the material world and the natural laws that govern it. We have talked about *Vahhd* – the totality of natural law – that governs all of the material world. *Vahhd* is all-encompassing and all-powerful. At least it is according to SciGen. *Vahhd* is ever-present. This has become our 'Absolute Truth': that there is a material world governed by natural law, intimately tied to logic. Perhaps we cannot rule out that natural law may have failed at some time in the past. There are those who believe that miracles are just those moments when natural law has failed. So be it. This does not detract from the truth we believe, that there is a material world and that natural law and logic play an intimate role in its behavior. It is simply impossible to escape this.

Although the dimension and magnitude of the material world is truly the measure of our lives, it is now time to recognize that the material world is not the only world that exists. The next step on our journey comes with the realization that there is a world beyond or outside of the material. We will call this the world of the *unseen*, or that which cannot be seen. The unseen world is a cornerstone of our spiritual identity and understanding.

Let's clarify what we mean by these two worlds: *the seen and the unseen*. In deference to our concept of science, we call the material world the *seen* world. We don't mean this literally, that all aspects of the material world are visible in the traditional sense. What we mean is that the material world can be sensed, perhaps by sight but also by other senses (hearing, touch, smell). Scientists base their worldview on the idea that properties of the material world can be measured. These measurements may involve something like 'sight', for example taking an image of a planet or other natural body. Or the measurements may involve something else, such as measuring the weight of an object. In either case, the material world is measurable and sensible. We call this the world of the *seen*.

If the natural world were all that existed, it is fair to say that all that exists would be *seeable* in this larger sense. We know that the natural world exists because we can measure something about it. This is, in fact, a hallmark of the scientific method. A scientific theory must be testable by experiment, so the objects of science need to be measurable in some way. The measurement may be direct or it may be indirect. For example, the way atoms were discovered was not by someone seeing them directly with his/her eyes. Atoms were discovered by the effect they had on sophisticated scientific instruments. Scientists inferred, using logic, that atoms must exist even though no one had actually seen one directly with their eyes. It is analogous to knowing there is a fire behind the door when you see smoke billowing out beneath it, and feeling the heat on the door.

The world of the seen is something very familiar to us. It is the material world we experience every moment of our lives. What then could I mean by the world of the *unseen*? It is quite different from the seen world. Whereas the seen world can be measured and sensed by our eyes and ears, the unseen world is beyond our direct sensory perception. But if we cannot 'sense' it (not see it, nor touch it, nor smell it), how do we know it exists? That is an important subject we shall discuss in this chapter. *For the world of the unseen must exist, as surely as you or I exist.*

It would be natural at this point to believe the following: science treats as its subject the *seen*, whereas the *unseen* is not within the province of science. It is this sort of thinking that leads some 'true believers' in science to declare that only science is the way to truth, because science deals exclusively with the *seen*. It is comforting for these believers to think that scientific knowledge is on the firmest of foundations because it is 'backed up' by actual measurements, measurements that are without ambiguity and without doubt. Even today, I hear some of my scientist friends accept science and reject religion because science is based on the firm foundation of 'real' measurement. Religion, on the other hand, is derived from truths that are not measured, truths that must be passed down or 'revealed' by a higher power. These religious truths, it is claimed, are less reliable or believable than truths based on measurements. Measurements are something that I can see, that are objectively 'out there' in the real world. Measurements, it is said, are the most solid foundation for truth.

There is a fallacy in this thinking, and it has led many astray. Yes, it is reasonable to believe in the seen world and the world of science. As we have discussed, many important truths lie there. The fallacy is to believe that scientific truth is exclusively in the province of the seen. Measurements, tangible and real as can be, are important to science. But science cannot escape the world of the *unseen*. Science is not just about the world of the seen, but about the unseen world also. Therefore, if you reject the unseen as being a lower order of truth, and less reliable, then you cannot escape that science itself may be on a less firm foundation than you originally thought. The scientific and religious paths towards truth may be more similar than you imagine.

The existence of the seen and unseen worlds is important to our journey because we will learn that both are vitally important to our humanity. Neither world alone is sufficient: humans must inhabit both worlds. Our quest for meaning and our hunger for spiritual truth are bound up with both the seen and unseen worlds. As humans, we cannot deal with only one or the other.

It is now time to describe the world of the unseen.

The Unseen World

We have talked a great deal about something we have not yet described! What is the unseen world? We can say this about it:

> *The unseen world cannot be measured.* It is 'beyond measure' and not subject to scientific analysis in the traditional sense.
>
> *The unseen world is eternal and ever-present.* The unseen knows no bound due to physical limitations or limited dimension in time or space. The unseen world is infinite.
>
> *The unseen world is intimately bound up with our humanity.* We cannot be human without a strong bond to the world of the unseen.

In my own thinking about the seen and the unseen, I use a simple concept to distinguish between the two worlds. If I am trying to decide whether something resides in the world of the seen or the unseen, I ask myself a very simple question: *does it have mass?* According to science, all material things have mass. (Sometimes, material things have zero mass, but zero is still a legitimate value.) If something is in the world of the seen – in the material world – it has mass. Conversely, *things in the unseen world have no mass.* It is not that the mass is zero, which in fact is a legitimate value for the mass of an object (as long as it moves at the speed of light). It is that mass itself cannot be defined or measured for the thing. The concept of mass makes no sense for things in the unseen world. If there is no way to define the mass of something, then I know that that thing, whatever it is, does not exist in the material world.[1]

It is easiest to describe the unseen world by way of an example. Let's imagine two objects sitting on a table; for example, two apples. The apples are material things. They exist in the material world and can be the subject of scientific investigation. They have mass. There are many scientific facts about apples. Let's turn our attention from the apples to the fact that there are two of them. That is something related to the apples that we might notice immediately. The fact that there are two apples is not a property of the apples themselves. There just happens to be two apples.

There being two apples is an example of the apples fitting into a pattern, the pattern I will call 'two-of-something'. We would all notice that pattern if we saw the apples sitting there. We would all know there are *two of them*. Let's now remove the apples and substitute rocks in their place. There are now two rocks sitting on the table. Although rocks are very different from apples, something is similar between these two situations: two apples or two rocks on a table. The commonality between these two situations is that the apples and the rocks both fit the pattern called 'two-of-something'. Two apples and two rocks are both specific examples of the pattern 'two-of-something'. Two apples and two rocks are very different things. But they both fit the pattern 'two-of-something', so there is something common about these two situations that transcends the differences between apples and rocks.

Let us focus on the pattern. What can we say about the 'two-of-something' pattern? There are many, many different kinds of things that fit that pattern. Anytime I can identify 'two-of-something' in a situation, I've got another example of the 'two-of-something' pattern. Two apples, two cars, two quarks, two electrons, etc., etc. Does the pattern exist outside of the objects that fit the pattern? Of course it does. We can talk about the pattern, refer to it, think about it, even like it! The pattern exists, even if the objects themselves are nowhere to be found.

I now want to ask another question: does the pattern exist in the material world? Can I measure the pattern? *Does the pattern 'two-of-something' have mass?* No, it does not. There is no way to assign a mass to the pattern 'two-of-something'. I am not saying that the pattern has a mass of zero. The pattern does *not* travel at the speed of light either. Rather, the idea of mass applied to a pattern makes no sense. The question 'What is the mass of that pattern?' makes no sense. Therefore, the pattern 'two-of-something' does not exist in the material world. *The pattern is part of the world of the unseen.*

'Two-of-something' is just one example of a pattern, a very simple one. We can all think of other patterns, such as 'three-of-something', or 'on-top-of-something' or 'bigger-than-something'. We all know how this works. The point we don't think about too often is that patterns are very real, but they aren't part of the material world. We forget this, because we usually recognize patterns in connection with objects in the material world. We forget that the patterns themselves *transcend* the material world. The patterns are not material objects.

Patterns have a lot to do with the unseen world that I am referring to. Patterns are very simple. We all know what we mean by them. Is that all there is to the world of the unseen? When I first started discussing the unseen, you may have thought I was describing something exotic and otherworldly, something secret that only a few could understand. Now I am saying that the world of the unseen is the world associated with patterns. Patterns are simple. How could something so simple be useful to us on our spiritual journey?

Patterns are simple, but they are also profound. For much of the rest of this book, we will be exploring how the simple idea of patterns affects us very profoundly. The reason is that patterns are a window into the world of the unseen, which transcends time and space. As such, patterns are not the object of scientific inquiry. But science depends critically upon patterns, and cannot exist without them. Therefore, science is not only about the seen. Science is about the seen and unseen, the measurable and unmeasurable.

Patterns are profound for another reason. As human beings, we are intimately involved with them. Humans have a unique capacity to understand patterns and react to them. More importantly, patterns affect us profoundly. They affect how we live and work, our happiness and our grief. Patterns are a window into our spiritual world. To continue on this journey, you will need to become more familiar with patterns, and how they affect us. That is what we discuss next.

The Unseen and You

Patterns are very real and very important. Yes, they exist outside of the material world. Patterns exist outside of nature. As human beings, we are uniquely qualified to understand such things.

I have already presented a very simple example of a pattern: the *two-ness* of something. There are other such examples, such as *three-ness* (obvious), or 'on top of' or 'behind'. Patterns can also encompass much more interesting things, such as love, marriage and joy. When I say love is a pattern, I mean the idea of love. If we acknowledge the idea of love, and talk to each other about it, we need not be referring to a specific instance of love in the real world. We are referring to the idea of love, which is a form of pattern.

Let's step back for a minute and think about this: *an idea is a kind of pattern*. This may not make much sense to you, and you might not even agree with it. I will soon give you a very specific way in which ideas and patterns are related, but before I do that, let's think about the implications. *An idea is a kind of pattern*. Just like patterns, ideas do not occupy a specific time or place. They are not 'tied down' to the material world as we know it. Ideas can exist independently of those who think of them. They have an existence of their own: we can identify them and talk about them, refer to them, remember them and forget them. They certainly exist, but I can't point to a location where an idea exists. An idea is outside the material world. That's also what we said about patterns.

Ideas have no mass. Modern science cannot assign a mass to an idea, or even define the concept of the 'mass' of an idea. Therefore, ideas are not part of the material world, since science tells us that all material things have mass. This is very similar to patterns: patterns have no mass either. Neither patterns nor ideas occupy a specific region of space, nor do they have a lifetime. Patterns are eternal, and so are ideas. This we know because the vagaries of the material world cannot affect them. They are outside of it.

Ideas According to SciGen

SciGen provides us with another way to understand the relationship between patterns and ideas. SciGen provides a very specific notion of what an idea is. Ideas happen within the brains of people who think of them. You and I might be talking about love, so we both have an idea of what love means (undoubtedly, the idea will differ between us). SciGen tells us that the idea of love happens inside your brain as a pattern of *neurons* firing in your brain. The pattern of neurons firing represents in some way the idea of love. Neurons are the basic building blocks of the brain, sort of like wires and transistors in a computer chip. Different ideas correspond in our brains to different patterns of neurons and the way they 'fire' as we think.

In SciGen, the relationship between ideas and patterns is this: ideas are patterns of neurons firing in the brain. Let's consider two people discussing love in some way. Both of these people must have an idea of what love is. The idea of love arises in the brains of the two people talking about it. Although the idea of love is common to each person, it is certainly different brains that are thinking about a similar idea. Physically distinct brains are representing in some way the same idea. This happens because of *patterns*. The neurons in each person's brain are of course different between the two people. They don't share the same brain! But if both people are thinking about the same idea – love – then there is something in common within the brains of these two people as they talk to each other. What they have in common is the pattern of how the neurons are firing. The neurons themselves are not common. (I say the patterns are similar between these two people because human brains largely share the same structure between different people. Since the brains of two people are not exactly the same, the pattern of neurons firing must be different also, even if these two people are thinking about the same idea. That's OK. The patterns don't have to be exactly the same for us to understand what is happening.)

As we said, according to SciGen, the connection between ideas and patterns is that ideas are patterns of neurons firing in the brain. What has this to do with you? This fact suggests something very important: that people are intimately connected to patterns. When we think and feel, we are connecting in a very fundamental way to patterns. Patterns can be shared by everyone, and do not know time and place, or limitation. Patterns do not need to eat to survive, and cannot die. Patterns are immortal. Being connected to patterns means I am connected in some way to the eternal.

Patterns are infinite, transcendent and eternal. Why should I care about that? My intimate connection to patterns means that, as a human being, I am intimately connected to a world that is infinite, transcendent and eternal. This is a tremendous gift! *Praise be to the creator for this gift!* People have an amazing ability to connect with an eternal and transcendent world. An analogy you can think of is the antenna of a radio. We connect to the transcendent world as if we possess an antenna that can sense a world outside the material world. Our antenna is a spiritual one, which connects to a world outside of the material world. We have a direct channel to the world of the spirit. We sense it, know it, and act on it, every minute of our lives that we have awareness. Our 'spiritual radio' is the key to our fulfillment as human beings.

You might be thinking that the spiritual antenna is not real. It is very real and completely aligned with the scientist's worldview. How can our brain connect us to a non-material world that is outside the realm of science? It can, because the brain creates and reacts to ideas. The physical structure of our brain actually changes based on ideas and thoughts that we have. It is truly an amazing thing.

According to SciGen, ideas are patterns of neurons firing. Neurons make up the physical structure of our brain. As we think and have ideas, we are changing the way those neurons fire. If we remember an idea, then a long-lasting change to our brain structure has occurred. If you have ever had a thought that is memorable, that has affected you and made you feel something different, then you probably remember that idea. Remembering the idea means that your brain has been changed from that moment onward. The *physical structure* of your brain has changed, and it has changed in response to an *idea*. That is, a pattern begets change in the material world. *The eternal world has effected change in the material world.* Our antenna to the spiritual world creates these changes.

Our spiritual antenna is our profound connection to the world of the unseen, the world that is beyond science. I want to emphasize that this connection is completely compatible with SciGen. Our current understanding of how people are affected by patterns and ideas is a scientific truth, not a revealed truth. This is one way that science leads us down a fruitful spiritual path. Science has given us insight into a connection we have to an eternal world, a world that is beyond science. How can I benefit from this knowledge? That is something we discuss next.

Understanding Your Spiritual Antenna

At this point you might be thinking: spirituality according to SciGen is not interesting. Maybe it's not even correct: are SciGen and spirituality really connected? After all, spirituality is a part of religious beliefs. Religion is what fills you with hope, helps you understand right from wrong, and prepares you for an eternal afterlife. SciGen reduces everything to the brain, to the patterns of neurons as they fire. Neurons are just slimy things that exist inside your skull. How can this be enlightening compared to religion?

If that is your opinion, you are certainly correct in this respect: yes, SciGen can only offer seemingly mundane perspectives on spirituality. In SciGen, ideas are part of brain function, and brains are made of slimy neurons. *SciGen cannot escape reducing everything to the material world.* SciGen is about things that have mass, like the brain. SciGen connects everything, even the ideas inside our heads, to their material aspect.

Yet, we also know there is a world beyond the material one. This unseen world contains the things that have no mass. SciGen is about the material world, but it does not rule out the spiritual one. As we've discussed, the scientific method itself relies on the unseen world because science relies on concepts. It is not contradictory to be a believer in SciGen and yet be aware of and in awe of the spiritual. SciGen in fact demands that material and spiritual worlds co-exist.

What has this to do with you? It has lots to do with you if you have a spiritual hunger in your heart. The fundamental reality of our lives is that, as humans, we have a unique understanding of, and sensitivity to, the non-material world. We transcend the material world. In this transcendence, science can provide guidance, but the guidance is limited. Science can provide the 'big picture' to us, which is: the material world is governed by natural laws, and logic is a key part of those laws. Science also tells us that there is a world beyond the material. SciGen shows us the character of natural law, and that natural law only governs part of this world, but not all of it. The world of the unseen is not governed by natural law.

SciGen tells us also that the material world is transient and mortal. Everything in the material world is subject to transformation. Living things are transformed by the natural laws that govern all material things, and they eventually die.

On the other hand, the unseen world has a currency in the immortal. The unseen does not die, because it transcends time and space. Natural law does not act on the unseen. This is important, because our human ability to connect to the unseen world means we can connect to an eternal world of immortal things. That is what makes our 'spiritual antenna' so valuable: we connect to the immortal, and part of us becomes immortal in the process. Cherish this gift.

Our next step is to increase our understanding of the 'big picture' that SciGen has revealed to us. We shall explore, by thinking and reflecting, what our relationship is to the spiritual world. We will come to realize that the material world and the spiritual world must be explored in different ways. We will find lessons from the material world that lead to our spiritual growth. We will also understand the limitations of science in guiding our spiritual natures. We must look elsewhere than science, often and continuously. To be fully human, we must go beyond the seen world, beyond the things that have mass. The material world is only a small part of our human universe. That is the blessing bestowed upon us. We must fulfill our destiny with the unseen.

5

Spirituality: The Right and the Wrong

To proceed along our spiritual path, we must discuss the idea of right and wrong. All religions instruct on right and wrong because morality is central to a life of the spirit. You cannot be spiritually whole without a moral compass. You cannot be fully human without it. By 'moral compass' we mean some understanding of the difference between right and wrong. To understand this difference, you must have some idea of what right is, and what wrong is.

We will discuss in this chapter how morality is viewed from the perspective of physical science. Science is about the material world, the world of things with mass, and not directly about the world of ideas of right and wrong.

Yet, we will find that science, and the story of SciGen, has much to teach us about right and wrong. What science teaches us about morality is indirect. We will need to fill in the details using resources *outside* of science. Science will not provide us with commandments. Science will not tell us what is morally right and wrong.

Science can teach us many things that advance our understanding of morality. In particular, science teaches that morality is an act of faith. Morality is not something that presents itself as a consequence of natural law or of *Vahhd*. The material world presents no moral code to us, so every time we make a moral decision we are partaking in the unseen world. Morality is outside the realm of the material. Morality is based on faith and belief. That alone is a lesson worth learning.

There are those who believe that the modern scientific world has led to a decline in moral values. Some say that science and modernity lead to moral 'relativism', meaning that right and wrong depends on your point of view. And yet, surely we long for a world where there is right and wrong, because a world without right and wrong is too horrible to contemplate. If we cannot rely on science, where can we turn for moral guidance? We must turn to the world of the unseen. This is the powerful message that we must learn, and science can help us learn it. The world of morality exists totally distinct from the world of *Vahhd*, distinct from the material world of transitory existence and casting-off. Morality's place is in the world of eternal things.

Many are resigned to believe that moral relativism is an inevitable consequence of our modern world, even as they yearn for moral guidance and strength. So many people are quietly desperate, appreciating modernity and standing in awe of it, yet lamenting its inevitable path down an amoral road. Yet, there is hope. We need not be resigned to a world of moral decay. Science does not preclude a strong sense of values as part of our spiritual core.

Why Be Moral in a Scientific World?

It is easy to understand how the modern scientific world has led to the perception that all morality is 'relative'. The reason is this: science has 'dethroned' our creator, and led people to seek other answers in the world. As people turn away from God, people turn away from the moral authority. This is an important point that you should remember: that moral authority is handed down from God. Some would say, 'revealed' from God. The moral authority tells us what is right and what is wrong. Losing our moral authority means we have lost the sense of right and wrong, which is the same as saying that morality is relative.

Yet, the need for a moral sense has not vanished. Even the most die-hard atheists will acknowledge that there is a right and a wrong. To be human, we need a moral path to follow. In SciGen, what is the source of morality? We have seen that in the Scientific

Genesis story, there is no mention of a God and no mention of 'goodness' or 'badness'. Do believers in SciGen have no sense of right and wrong? That is certainly not true, but the source of right and wrong in SciGen is certainly different from what it is in religion. That is what we will discuss next. This is what you must remember: in religion, right and wrong is revealed to us from God. In SciGen, right and wrong are determined differently.

SciGen and Morality: The Importance of Psyche

What is the source of right and wrong in SciGen? As we have discussed, science is not a direct way to learn about right and wrong. Scientific theories do not contain moral messages or commandments. The concepts of right and wrong are not material things. If you think of right and wrong as concepts or ideas, then you already know that moral concepts have no mass. Moral concepts lie outside of direct scientific inquiry (we remind the reader that we are always referring to physical science). However, the concepts of right and wrong are compatible with SciGen. Moral concepts do not violate fundamental tenets of SciGen nor pose a threat to the consistency of scientific reasoning.

If we turn towards science and away from God, and doubt the morality that God has given us, what takes its place? Before we discuss this, I want to manage your expectations regarding what can be said about SciGen and morality. SciGen permits us to state general things about morality. Science cannot reveal to us that a particular act or decision is right or wrong. The scientific method does not permit us to derive a specific moral code. What we will do in this chapter is reveal the ways that people have tried to develop moral codes starting with SciGen. All these efforts must go outside of science to succeed. Yet, these efforts are done with science as a primary worldview. What you will learn is that, in SciGen, morality tends to focus on something I will call the human *psyche*. I will describe the psyche in more detail further on. For now, just think of it as 'mind'.

It should not surprise you that the human psyche (or human mind) plays a major role in discussions of morality. In the big picture, SciGen consists of two central elements: the material world, and the world of concepts. The latter requires human thought. Even the most die-hard SciGen believer knows that morality must involve human thought in some way. But within SciGen itself, there is no need for God. Therefore, moral theories that rely heavily on scientific thinking find the human mind or psyche to be their principal source of moral guidance.

We now explain how the psyche plays a critical role in morality. There are basically two ways to derive a moral code: one way is from God. God is the source of the moral code and communicates it to us in some way. As good, moral people, we should abide by God's commandments. Another way to derive a moral code is from ideas that may be divorced from God. Some would say that a moral *philosophy* can be divorced from God. A moral code divorced from God depends strongly on the moral philosophy and beliefs that people develop for themselves.

That brings us to psyche. If a moral code emanates from the human mind, then we need to understand the mind in order to understand how that moral code is formed. We will now put a name on a moral code that is *not* revealed from God. We call this *psyche-based morality*, or PBM for short. (Making acronyms for things is something that scientists do a lot of!) PBM is the kind of morality that is *very* compatible with SciGen. Many scientists, particularly atheists, probably believe in some form of PBM. Given what you already know about SciGen, it should not surprise you that to understand PBM better we need to talk about the human mind or psyche. This we do next.

SciGen and Psyche: The Need for Brain

According to SciGen, the human mind is what emerges from the human brain. This may seem like a silly and overly simplistic statement, but we need to be very clear about it. In SciGen, the human mind is the result of activities, dynamics, chemistry, biology and physics, happening within the human brain. Mind comes from natural law (*Vahhd*) acting on the material brain, which consists of brain cells, molecules and chemicals. Yes, *brains have mass*.

Let's be very clear about the SciGen perspective. *Mind* is not a purely physical thing. Mind must involve ideas and thoughts in some way, concepts that are not the direct subjects of scientific inquiry (concepts have no mass). However, in SciGen, the ideas and thoughts that make up mind are patterns of neurons and other structures in the brain. The neurons etc. are strictly physical things subject to scientific inquiry. The patterns produced by these neurons help to make up 'mind'. We're in a middle ground here. Mind cannot exist without neurons, yet neurons alone do not define mind. The patterns made by neurons help complete the picture.

Knowing something about the brain will help us understand something about PBM, because of the way that brain and mind are tied together. We won't get too complicated here, nor will we try to describe everything that scientists have learned scientifically over the past few hundred years about the brain. Rather, we will distill what has been learned scientifically to a very simple picture that ignores lots of details but captures the essentials of what we need to know.

> *Aside:* scientists often use simplified models to help them under-stand a physical system that is actually more complicated. That's OK, if the model captures essential features of the complicated system and helps us understand it. An example is a baseball. Baseballs are actually quite complicated things at the atomic level, but one does not need to consider atoms at all when describing how a baseball moves through the air.

SciGen and Psyche: The Pleasure Center

According to SciGen, moral philosophies that come from *mind* must be related in some way to a physical *brain* (brains have *mass*). What scientists have learned over the years is that the human brain has at least one area within it called a *pleasure center*. This area of the brain tends to be active when people are experiencing a pleasurable sensation. We will use these scientific observations to consider a simple model of the brain that will help us understand psyche-based morality.

The first pleasure-center experiments found that animals would stimulate their pleasure centers instead of eating, and would in fact starve themselves if given the choice. Later experiments with humans showed that certain addicting drugs stimulate the brain's pleasure center. Drugs release chemicals in the brain that stimulate the pleasure center. It was later found that food and sex stimulate the pleasure center also. These initial experiments raise an intriguing possibility: what if the pleasure center is stimulated when people feel generally happy, or perceive something as morally 'good'? Scientists don't yet know if happiness or goodness is related to the same pleasure center that activates when we eat. We will ignore that distinction. For now, it is useful for us to imagine that happiness, goodness and feelings of fulfillment are related to activation of a pleasure center in our brain. This simplified picture or *model* of the brain is not exactly correct, but it will help us understand psyche-based morality. This simple model allows us to understand the connection between *mind* and *brain*.

With our concept of the pleasure center, we are closer to under-standing how psyche-based morality works. Let's consider a simple example. The pleasure center is activated when certain things happen in the outside world as captured by our senses. Let's consider the example of eating food when we are hungry. As the molecules of food enter our mouth, a series of physical events and chemical reactions happens in our bodies, leading to our pleasure center being stimulated. That means that a certain group of neurons (the pleasure center) in our brain gets stimulated. When this happens, we feel 'pleased'. We are happy to be eating the food!

After all, we were hungry. In this simple example, we have connected a physical region of the brain to a much more complicated property of our minds called 'pleasure'. So be it. That is where scientific knowledge today leads us.

Psyche-based morality can follow a similar sequence of events in some respects. Let's work out a specific case. Suppose we are walking down the street and we pass a little baby, wrapped in blankets and crying on a doorstep. It appears to us that the baby was left there and is in distress. We call the police and they immediately dispatch someone from child services to help the baby, picking it up and comforting it. Although we are distressed about why a baby was abandoned, we know that now the baby is in good hands. We perceive the enhanced safety of the baby as a good thing. We think: 'Rescuing the baby is a good thing.' What we mean is: good in a *moral* sense. We all know instinctively that leaving a defenseless baby on a doorstep to uncertain peril and harm is a bad thing (morally bad). Almost any normal adult person would have done the same thing: try to help a defenseless baby. Helping defenseless babies is morally 'good', almost everyone would agree.

Let's break this down a little more, using our pleasure-center model of the brain. Our sensory organs (seeing and hearing) send signals to our brain that we interpret with our brain and our mind. We perceive a bad situation regarding the baby, so we try to correct it, make it right. We try to create a better situation by calling the authorities. When the authorities come and offer help, we are pleased. Therefore, the pleasure-center part of our brain is stimulated when we see the baby getting help. Of course, what's really happening is more complicated. For our discussion here, these extra complications don't matter. What does matter is that the brain has been activated in such a way that we perceive the baby being protected. We perceive that protection as a 'good' situation. I am sure that the real reactions in our brain are more complicated that I have described. The details do not concern us. The gist of the idea is this: our sensory organs lead to a series of chemical and physical reactions in the brain that lead to the stimulation of the brain's pleasure center. In our example, the stimulation results from something we perceive to be morally good. In the case of eating food, the stimulation results for other reasons. These two cases differ, but in many respects they are similar.

You might think at this stage that I am trying to simplify human morality too much. Is it really similar to pleasure from food or other sensory pleasures? No, I am not trying to oversimplify something as rich and complex as human morality. I am not trying to say that deciding what is morally good or morally bad is the same thing as deciding what foods are good or bad. I am saying that psyche-based morality puts these two things on a somewhat equal basis, although they differ in complexity. Certainly, psyche-based morality is more complex than deciding what foods are good or bad. There are similarities, however. The similarity has to do with how we perceive or decide what is good. For psyche-based morality, deciding what is good is based on what we'll call 'brain-state'. Brain-state is the detailed configuration of your brain: the pattern of neurons in your brain, the chemical and electrical connections between the neurons and all the physics that goes along with that. You can think of brain-state as a snapshot of the atoms and molecules in your brain and how they are interacting at some instant. It is what your brain is at any given instant (and it changes instant to instant).

In PBM, when you perceive something to be morally good, that perception must in some way be connected to 'brain-state'. We have simplified brain-state to a pleasure-center model of the brain. (That oversimplified model is good enough for the purposes of this discussion.) So, in PBM, perceiving something as morally good means that that perception has stimulated your brain's pleasure center. Similarly, good food stimulates the brain's pleasure center. That is the connection between 'good food' and 'morally good'. In both cases, a part of your brain has been stimulated in a certain way to produce the perception of 'goodness'. Although 'good food' and 'morally good' are completely different things, in SciGen they are related by the fact that they both essentially involve physical conditions within your brain. We perceive goodness in both these things, and that perception is tied to our brain-state.

I hope the previous discussion has helped you to understand psyche-based morality. Psyche-based morality is the type of morality most compatible with SciGen because PBM is heavily rooted in the material world and natural law. I am not claiming that PBM is the 'correct' morality, or that most people today believe in it. Nor am I claiming that all scientists believe in it or should. A key fact is that PBM does not require religious ideas such as a personal God. PBM makes the connection between morality and brain, and brain is what is responsible for the human psyche (according to SciGen).

Now that we've broken it down, let's try to understand the implications of PBM. According to SciGen, PBM is strongly tied to our brains. What are the implications?

The Good and the Bad: What is Possible in Psyche-Based Morality

Before further discussion of psyche-based morality, let's step back and look at the big picture. Perhaps you are reading about PBM for the first time and are uncomfortable about tying moral beliefs to the physical and chemical structure of your brain. Let's ponder that: morality is related to chemical and physical reactions in the brain. Is this just a bad science-fiction story? How is such a thing possible? Isn't morality a much more profound and important thing than that? Many of you reading this book no doubt believe in the sanctity and centrality of morality to our lives. You might be offended by a concept such as PBM, particularly if you believe that God is the source of our moral code. So be it. It is not my intention to sway your beliefs. I am merely trying to help you understand PBM because it is so closely tied to SciGen.

Those who believe that SciGen is a sufficient basis for morality probably believe in some version of PBM. Your moral views may be based on religion, and differ significantly from PBM. If so, it is still worth learning about PBM to understand the 'other side' of the moral argument. Every moral code presents opportunities and challenges to our understanding and beliefs. If your moral code is based on religion, do not close your mind to ways of understanding that differ from your own. Listen first to the 'other' way, so that you may better explain and justify your faith in something better.

A striking feature of PBM is that it is a moral code tied to a material thing we call the human brain (so it is according to SciGen). You may find this acceptable or you may find this repugnant. It is certainly *different* from deriving a moral code from a higher power such as God. God is the ultimate moral authority who reveals to us, his creation, what is right and what is wrong. Deriving right and wrong from the human psyche is vastly different from that. One difference is that morality emerging from the psyche is strongly tied to its material source, the brain. In PBM, what we believe to be right and wrong depends on the perceptions we form within our brains. As our brains change, which happens for any number of reasons, so will our morals change. This leads to a form of 'moral relativism', which means that morality is not absolute but rather changes depending on what people believe. Beliefs and culture are always changing, therefore so will our moral views. That's inherent in PBM.

Belief in morals descending from a higher power would appear to be less changeable or relative than PBM. Many have received their moral instruction from a source such as a holy book, which they believe is the revealed truth of God, the one true moral authority. A written code is passed down from God to form the foundation of our moral beliefs. This foundation would seem less subject to change than PBM, which is based on a material object: the human brain. The timeless nature of revealed morality and truth is very appealing to many people, in contrast to the more 'relative' moral truth of PBM. Revealed truth has been written down and originates from a source we believe to be authoritative. In contrast, PBM is not revealed from a higher power. PBM is dependent on the changing material world. For PBM, there is no 'absolute moral authority' which one is compelled to believe.

Another feature of PBM is that it might be a 'looser' form of morality than is revealed morality. That is because what is considered 'good' in PBM has to make us *feel good* in some way. Whereas deeply religious people may subject themselves to physical and emotional deprivation to enhance their souls or connection to God, such deprivation is less likely to be part of PBM. If God tells us that sacrifice is good for us, then our faith tells us to accept that sacrifice and improve ourselves by listening to God and denying ourselves certain pleasures in life. It's harder to fit self-denial and self-deprivation into a moral code based on psyche. It's not impossible, but it's not as easy to see it. So, believers in PBM will probably be more comfortable with physical pleasures than some who believe in revealed morality, at least in general.

Although there appears to be a wide gulf between PBM and revealed (religious) moral truth, the gulf need not be as wide as it first appears. Remember that the central theme of this book is to reveal how science can help us lead more spiritual lives. An important part of spirituality has to do with the moral sphere. Understanding PBM can help us be better people, whether we are believers in God or SciGen. Certainly, the difference between PBM and revealed morality is fundamental and must remain. But we can, at the same time, learn from the scientific view, which is at the core of PBM. We'll discuss that next.

SciGen and the Good

If I told you I know a group of believers in SciGen who are morally resolute, among the most moral people I know, you might not believe me. Did we not just describe how SciGen leads to moral relativism? Isn't relative morality a loose set of moral codes, looser than morality revealed from a higher power? Shouldn't believers in SciGen be morally 'looser' than those who practice religion? Perhaps in general this is true. But it need not be that way. We will describe next some of the surprising implications of SciGen's psyche-based morality.

To understand how moral behavior emerges from psyche-based morality, we need to recall the steps that lead to a moral code within SciGen. It goes like this: we start with the material world (*seen* world), which is a central element in SciGen. The human brain is the material system where perceptions of moral good and bad occur. Moral perceptions ('I feel this is a good thing to do...') are the result of patterns and interactions among neurons in the brain. We have focused on neurons that reside in the brain's pleasure center. If the pleasure center becomes stimulated after we witness a certain act or deed, then we may perceive that deed to be morally 'good'. In this way, what is good and bad is decided based on how parts of our brain are stimulated.

Although this description of psyche-based morality invokes a simplified model of how the brain works, the model can aid our understanding. In SciGen, the structure of neurons and their firing patterns are key to perceiving an act as good or bad. Certain deeds that many of us would consider immoral deeds might not necessarily be considered immoral in SciGen. It depends on how the neural patterns are firing within the physical structure of the brain. Let's return to the example of the defenseless baby, except that we change the scenario. Suppose that we could construct brains for which the pleasure center is stimulated when babies are being threatened. People with those brains are more likely to believe that harming babies is morally good.

This 'moral relativism' can work *both ways* in SciGen. A striking fact is that a high degree of morality is also compatible with SciGen. There are people who simply do not feel tempted to sin. Using our pleasure center model, we would say that potentially sinful activities do not stimulate the pleasure center of these individuals. Such people feel less temptation and earn a certain immunity from sin. Another possibility is that, for these 'good' people, their pleasure center is stimulated by the knowledge that they have *resisted* sin. Perhaps you or someone you know is like that: they just seem to resist all manner of temptation and vice; they follow the straight and narrow, content in their righteous ways. Such righteousness is also compatible with SciGen.

Moral righteousness does not require belief in a personal God. To be righteous within SciGen requires only that certain physical conditions exist within the brain of the righteous person. The 'correct' brain structure will produce a righteous person. It can work every which way. Another brain structure will produce another form of morality. Morality is certainly relative within SciGen, but that does not mean that SciGen believers are morally bad.

We now understand why SciGen need not lead to 'looser' moral values. However, we cannot escape the fact that SciGen leads to moral relativism, because it is based on a material thing (the brain) that is changeable and transitory. The brain exists in the material world, not in the eternal unseen world.

If you believe in an 'absolute' morality, *then you are going beyond SciGen*. If you believe that certain things are sacred, such as the value of human life or protecting the innocent from harm, *then you are going beyond SciGen*. If you believe there are important moral values that should hold for all time and should be defended from the fashions of the moment, *then you are going beyond SciGen. What I mean is this: you have faith*. You have belief that there is morality that transcends the transitory physical world and reaches an eternal status. Only through such belief can you defend righteousness from the vagaries of the present, to achieve a view of right and wrong that is as solid as bedrock.

Be mindful that faith in right and wrong is truly going beyond

SciGen, but such faith is compatible with SciGen. Faith and SciGen can co-exist. Faith augments what SciGen can provide. Faith is the path to a stronger belief in the eternal right and the eternal wrong. Faith takes you farther down the moral road. You need not surrender to moral relativism once you find faith.

The Sin in SciGen

We have not yet discussed the concept of sin in SciGen. Can there be sin in SciGen? There can be wrongdoing, because in SciGen there is a concept of right and wrong. But can there be sin? The idea of sin carries with it a more permanent connotation than 'doing the wrong thing'. A true sinner will repeatedly do the wrong thing knowing full well that what he is doing is wrong. Certainly, in SciGen people can go against their own moral beliefs. One might ask why. Perhaps it is expediency or a temporary lust that causes the bad behavior. There are probably many reasons why a believer in psyche-based morality would violate that morality.

A deeper origin of sin in SciGen is ignoring Absolute Truth. Whereas in religion a sinner turns away from God, in SciGen a sinner turns away from, or ignores, the Absolute Truth. The SciGen sinner is one who acts as if there were no Absolute Truth. To do this, the sinner ascribes more power to themselves than they actually possess. This leads to all sorts of strife. In a future chapter we will describe how prayer and faith are the foundations of a spiritual life, even in SciGen. Most likely, a sinner in SciGen does not pray, and does not have the faith he or she needs to be fully spiritually aware.

6

Words

We have learned a great many things on our journey. The journey must be worth the effort; it must help us to live a better life. Now we are ready to make a personal connection between science and spirituality. We shall make this connection with words. For it is written: *'Man shall not live by bread alone, but by every word that proceedeth out of the mouth of God.'* Using words, we will become aware of the deep common ground shared by those who believe in God and those who believe in the Absolute Truth. May these words inspire you and give you hope.

'Everything we have is given to us'
Either the righteous person who fears God or the atheist who does not believe must know this: that everything we have is given to us. And from this we must be humble and pray that our lives are not lived in vain.

> Those who believe in God believe He is all-powerful: *'Be thou exalted, Lord God, in thine own strength: so will we sing and praise thy power.'* This infinite power has given us the creation and all things that follow. But what of those who do not believe? They too, must know that all we have is given to us. For we are all slaves to *Vahhd*. We do not control *Vahhd* but *Vahhd* controls us. Knowing this, so shall we be humble. So it must be with SciGen.

'Pray'
Prayer strengthens you and makes you whole. Prayer enriches your soul and leads you to greener pastures. For those who believe, it is truly written: *'Thus therefore shall you pray: Our Father who art in*

heaven, hallowed be thy name...' Prayer creates a bond between ourselves and the unfathomable mystery of our creation. Prayer is an acknowledgment that there are powers far greater than ourselves. This acknowledgment brings us closer to truth and to an understanding of our place in this world.

If you are of SciGen, why would you pray? I remember a fellow graduate student of mine, being an atheist, asking me 'Why should I pray?'

In prayer, we ask for help and guidance from a higher power. For believers, the higher power is God. In SciGen, the higher power is the laws of nature. But the laws of nature do not hear us, so why pray to them?

Even for non-believers, there is a reason to pray: to reaffirm our dependence on a higher power. We often forget how dependent we truly are. In our moments of greatest need and fearfulness, we feel alone and overwhelmed with our burdens and the choices that we face. It is comforting to know that what is destined will come to be. When we pray, we surrender ourselves to the higher power and are able to accept this truth: we cannot change our destiny. Managing to overcome our fears, and making the right choices despite fear, are acts of receiving guidance more so than acts of will.

'Every day, give thanks'

For we know that *everything we have is given to us*. All the blessings in your life have been given to you. And from whence did they come? From a power much greater than you. Give thanks for what you have received.

Believers know to give thanks to their true and merciful God: *'O give thanks unto the Lord; for he is good; for his mercy endureth for ever.'* And for what reason should non-believers give thanks? For what reason should they be grateful?

Because everything we have is given to us. We perceive ourselves to be the source of our own power and success, but in fact it comes from outside our control. We do not control ourselves, because 'we' do not control atoms or molecules or the laws of nature. In SciGen, atoms and molecules determine our actions, appetites and abilities. In SciGen, free will is an illusion. Therefore, be thankful for the blessings you have received.

You have a choice: to focus on the good in your life, or to focus on the bad. With faith as your guide, you can focus on the good. Know also that good things have been given to you from a power much greater than you.

'Forgive'

Why should you forgive those who have wronged you? *Because forgiveness frees your heart from hatred.* Hatred is a prison that embitters your soul. Know this: that forgiving is not weakness but a way to open your life to new possibilities.

Those who believe know that a merciful God forgives them as they should forgive others, for it is written: *'Forgive our trespasses as we forgive those who trespass against us.'*

In SciGen, the desire to forgive flows from an understanding of the world around us. Science teaches us that everyone is limited in their ability to influence their own views and behavior. Tolerance is a natural outcome of this understanding. In a strictly scientific view, we cannot blame the criminal for his crime for this criminal does not even control his will to do wrong. Yet we must assign a moral status to his act, through a process that involves faith. With our faith, we know the criminal has done wrong. Our scientific knowledge tells us that the criminal is trapped in a situation where he cannot help but do wrong. Therefore, let us duly punish those who do wrong, but with an eye to future forgiveness, if those who have done wrong honestly repent of their sins.

It was Jesus, in a time of great physical pain, who said of his perse-cutors: *'Forgive them, Father, for they know not what they do.'*

And know this also: every day, pray for forgiveness.

'Have no excesses of pride, but rather live your life with humility'

If all that we have is given to us, then why do we show excessive pride? Such pride is a falsehood. It is based on a false belief that we control more than we actually do. For it is written: *'When pride comes, then comes shame, but with humility comes wisdom.'* Be humble and thankful for what you have been given and for what you have achieved.

From where does the pride of non-believers come? It comes from a false idea that there is no God above them, and that their great achievements and talents stand above many things in the world. They believe that their talent and achievements create the path to their greatness. Yet, this book has shown us that our achievements and our talents emanate from forces beyond our control. These glorious things emanate from *Vahhd*.

Your talent and ability came from outside you, from a higher power which is not you. Accept this and rejoice, and do good works with your gifts, but do not be overly proud.

'Pray for wisdom'

Wisdom is one of the greatest of life's gifts that can be bestowed. Pray that you will be blessed with this gift. Wisdom will provide you with a deeper appreciation of your life and the world around you. Wisdom enhances life. Believers know that wisdom is a gift from God: *'But if any of you lacks wisdom, let him ask of God, who gives to all liberally and without reproach; and it will be given to him.'* Why should non-believers also pray for wisdom?

In SciGen, wisdom is a condition of your mind and your brain.

From whence does wisdom come, and how does one find it? Wisdom comes as a gift, not as a conscious act. You must be open to finding wisdom. For if you knew how to become wise, you would be wise already. Wisdom comes as you travel your journey. You embark on your journey before you know what you will find. Be open to receiving wisdom from your life's experiences and from others who help you. Pray that your mind remains open to receiving wisdom.

'And count this blessing also: that temptation has not found you'

Temptation touches everyone. Some are blessed with relatively few temptations. Others are cursed with heavy and dark temptations that lead them towards truly evil deeds. You must count yourself as blessed if you are free from the worst temptations. What is the difference between those who experience many temptations and those experiencing just a few minor ones? Believers know that experiencing relatively few temptations does not mark one as 'morally superior'. Believers know it is not their place to judge. This is left to God. Rather, believers continually rely on God to help them steer clear of the worst temptations, for it is written: *'Lead us not into temptation, but deliver us from evil.'*

According to SciGen, you do not control the temptations that befall you. *Vahhd* brings these temptations to you. If your temptations are harming you and those around you, you should honestly confront your limitations and be prepared to accept them. You should pray for healing and you should seek help. It is far worse to do evil deeds with no regard to your status as a sinner. You should accept the consequences of your actions. You should acknowledge your limitations and pray there is a path to regaining righteousness. *What a great blessing it is to be free of temptations!*

I hope you are able to appreciate the gift of righteousness, of being free of temptation. At the same time, do not be too harsh on those who cannot walk as straight a path as you. Although SciGen alone cannot fulfill our search for meaning, it can teach us to be more tolerant. A deeper understanding of the world around you, and knowing what you can and cannot control, will help you lead a more fulfilling and honest life. Learn to work towards positive goals and avoid being mired in the guilt of past sins.

'Nothing I have learned has convinced me to be less than generous, and less than loving'

What is the essence of love and generosity? Who are these that give of themselves freely with no expectation of material reward? Is this foolishness? No, it is certainly not that. Believers know that love and generosity brings us closer to God, for it is written: *'And if I have the gift of prophecy, and know all mysteries and all knowledge; and if I have all faith, so as to remove mountains, but have not love, I am nothing.'*

The scientific method and SciGen are 'value neutral', and cannot by themselves teach us to value generosity and kindness. Yet these virtues are fully compatible with a scientific worldview. From a scientific perspective, we will cherish these virtues if acting on these virtues stimulates our brain's pleasure center. Our brains are certainly 'hard-wired' to possess instincts other than love and generosity. We also tend to covet and envy. We may want more and more material things, seemingly without end. However, these wise words are written in the holy book: *'What does it profit a man to gain the world and lose his soul?'* You *can* learn to be more spiritual and less dependent on material pursuits. In SciGen, it is a matter of training your mind. The rewards are many. Ultimately, such training can enrich your life. Yet, you will feel emptiness if you do not have faith also. Do not forget or ignore faith. Faith is your foundation.

What are the benefits of love and generosity? It is nothing less than opening up a new world of spiritual joy. Generosity and love reorient your mind to find joy in the absence of material gain. Thus, you are finding joy by connecting to the eternal, spiritual world. Acting with generosity and love helps you develop your spiritual antenna, because it forces you to confront a world beyond the material. Generosity and love make no sense in a purely material calculation. You must go beyond that material logic. In doing so, you will open your mind and soul to new joyous possibilities.

For believers, there is another reason to be generous and loving. Such acts bring you closer to God.

'Deepest joy comes not through the eyes and ears, but through the spirit'

We have all experienced pleasure (and pain) from our senses, whether it be touch, taste or smell. You should be aware that a far deeper joy comes from your spirit, which is unconnected to material things. The spirit brings us a deeper sense of joy by touching our minds and our hearts. The senses cannot readily do this. For it is written: *'Ask, and you will receive, that your joy may be made full.'* And it is also written: *'Now may the God of hope fill you with all joy and peace in believing, that you may abound in hope, in the power of the Holy Spirit.'*

What can SciGen teach us about a deeper joy that comes through the spirit? SciGen puts no restriction on joy or its source, although many believe that SciGen leads one to embrace materialistic pleasures, pleasures that are more superficial than joy found through the spirit. The SciGen view is that joy is a mental state, reducible to patterns of neurons firing in one's brain. In SciGen, 'deep joy' arises from a connection between the brain's pleasure center and our thoughts – thoughts that may be separate from our senses. A believer in SciGen will make an explicit connection between the kingdom of heaven and 'mental states' associated with joy. The Bible says: *'The kingdom of heaven is like a treasure hidden in the field, which a man found, and hid. In his joy, he goes and sells all that he has, and buys that field.'* The Bible also states: *'For the kingdom of God is not eating and drinking, but righteousness, peace, and joy in the Holy Spirit.'* These connections between joy and righteousness, peace and heaven are interpreted within SciGen as statements of how the pleasure center can be stimulated by our thoughts. Such joy does not come from the senses, not even within SciGen.

The problem with joy within SciGen occurs when one reflects on the source of joy being experienced. Is joy simply 'brain states' or patterns of neurons? Such knowledge may in fact sap the joy dry. On the other hand, joy experienced in religion through faith is more robust, because it speaks of our connection to a higher being. Again, we see that faith is the center of our deepest and most vital life experiences. To experience the deepest joys, we must believe that our joys are rooted in more than chemical reactions. Faith infuses our joy with a deeper meaning. So it must be for the fullness of life to be experienced.

And it is written: *'For behold, the kingdom of God is within you.'*

'What does it profit a man to gain the world and lose his soul?'

This question is one of the most profound questions that we can ask ourselves. This question strikes at the essence of spirituality, righteousness and temptation. All of us have reached points in our lives when we wanted to have more 'things of this world', meaning material things and wealth. Have we sacrificed our 'soul' for those things? Have we compromised our values or our conscience to acquire material things? Have we forsaken spiritual vitality and growth for material gain? Have we sacrificed passionate belief to achieve material gain? These are all questions we must ask ourselves. Believers know that gaining material things does not bring us closer to God, and in fact can take us farther from God. Lies and sins we commit to achieve material gain separate us from God. You must ask yourself: is there anything in the material world worth enough to justify a greater distance between you and God?

In SciGen, material gain and spiritual gain are on nearly equal footing. The 'pleasure center model' of the brain teaches us that there are two ways of stimulating the pleasure center: with material pursuits, or with spiritual ones. We all know that material gain will profit you nothing if your soul is 'not in the right place'. There are many who have great material wealth and yet they feel their lives to be empty and lacking passion. Conversely, we are aware of those with little material wealth who seem to live a life of passion, connectedness and joy.

It does you no good to gain materially if such gain means that you are left spiritually bereft. Quiet moments of reflection are the time to remind ourselves of the spiritual blessings that we have, even if materially we are not as well off as we might have hoped. SciGen can help us understand that there is enormous value to what we possess spiritually. By your generosity and love you confirm your ability to experience spiritual joy.

SciGen teaches us another lesson also: that not everyone will be able to partake of spiritual riches. There are those who are blind to spiritual joy even if they have gained much materially. Many such people will never be 'saved' because they are unwilling or unable to experience a deeper spiritual joy. SciGen tells us that such deprived people simply have different wiring in their brains. There is little that can be done if they themselves do not try to become deeper and richer human beings.

Faith is the path towards fuller spiritual riches. Faith teaches us the value of spiritual enlightenment and of being close to God.

'You will know the truth, and the truth will make you free'
What is the relationship between truth and freedom? How will
knowing the truth make us free? Free from what? What truth is this
that will bring us freedom?

The truth of which we speak is *spiritual truth*. Such truth will
free you from a wretched search for the meaning of your life. Once
you know the truth – *that your life has a purpose and a meaning* – you
will feel a sense of enormous freedom as if a weight has been
removed from your shoulders. You will no longer feel a desperate
sense of helplessness and longing. You will no longer strive for
things that are vain. Knowledge of this truth brings you freedom
from spiritual want. Believers know that the purpose in their lives
comes through their faith in God.

In SciGen there is truth also, the Absolute Truth that is *Vahhd*.
Freedom comes from surrender to *Vahhd*. Once you recognize
your true place in the scheme of things, you will feel a sense of
exhilaration and freedom. The exhilaration comes from
knowing what you can control and what you cannot. You will
be freed from the burden of trying to change what you cannot
actually change. You will accept and surrender to those things
you cannot control. Such surrender brings freedom. You are no
longer responsible for those things! *Vahhd* is above you. You
cannot counter *Vahhd*! Anger and frustration melts away with
your resignation and acceptance of higher powers. You become
properly humble in the face of *Vahhd*. Knowing the truth will
realign you with the eternal.

And therefore I say: we are all slaves to *Vahhd*, but in our slavery
we shall be free. It is truly liberating to be a slave to righteousness.
Oh that I might know such sweet bondage! The truth of righteousness
is my freedom. And I pray that I may always walk this path of
surrender to righteousness.

'In your faith you will find the path of righteousness'

How do we know the right path to follow in our lives? Don't we wake up some mornings with a sense of unease and dread: what will become of me? What should I do with my energies and my passions, and what purpose do they serve? The answer is: the path you should follow is a righteous path, a path that respects creation and acknowledges a higher power in your life. By faith you will find this path.

In SciGen, acknowledging the Absolute Truth is a first step towards righteousness, but there is yet farther to go. For SciGen, the path to righteousness is in two steps. First, you must acknowledge the Absolute Truth and ponder what that means to you and to your life. Accept the sense of humility that comes from knowing the truth. Second, you must acknowledge the need for something beyond SciGen, that SciGen is not enough for you to find the right path. You must look elsewhere, beyond the material world to a world where perfection resides with the eternal. In SciGen alone, there is no path that brings true fulfillment. To be free of despair, you must acknowledge your need for faith.

'Treat others as you would wish them to treat you'

How should we treat others? What is the *right* way? Should we seek to take advantage of the weaknesses in our neighbors and friends, and derive as much personal benefit as possible from our relationships? Or, should we think of others first and try to give our friends and colleagues what they want, at the expense of what we want? The answer is that we should treat others as we would wish them to treat us. These simple words from the Bible contain a powerful message. To follow these words forces us to think about how we affect others. If what you plan to do is not what you would want done to you, reconsider your plan. Find a new plan that you would approve if done to you. That is the right way, and the way that will pay you benefits through eternity.

In SciGen, the Golden Rule ('Treat others as you would wish them to treat you') can be viewed as a statement born from logic. SciGen is 'value free' and value neutral. All people are of equal value in SciGen. Simply put: there is no scientific experiment that can reveal the value of a person, much less the relative value of two people. If you treat someone poorly, you cannot justify it within SciGen. By treating someone poorly, you put your needs above theirs and imply that you are more valuable than they. According to SciGen, such behavior is not justified.

The Golden Rule encourages the virtue of honesty. No one wants to be lied to. If you lie to others, then you are violating the Rule. Find a different way to meet your objectives, a way that does not require you to lie.

The mathematical logic of SciGen is compatible with the Golden Rule. That is a strength of SciGen. Yet, the Golden Rule born from SciGen is not uplifting of the spirit, because the SciGen version of the Golden Rule is not an affirmation of human value. Rather, the Golden Rule applies within SciGen because people have *no* intrinsic value. This is hardly a positive statement! Believers know that the Golden Rule is correct because God loves us all equally: we all have intrinsic worth as God's children. We should treat others well because they have intrinsic worth, as we ourselves do. It debases us when we treat others poorly. They deserve better and we should do better, as children of a benevolent and almighty creator. May your faith in the worth of human beings guide you towards righteous behavior towards others.

'All things of this world shall perish; yet faith endures'

SciGen teaches us that all things of this world shall perish. The material world is transitory and corrupt. Energy and matter constantly interact within the material world to bring about the demise of all we see now. Science is unequivocal on this point. Even the earth someday will be swallowed up by an expanding sun. Such has happened elsewhere in the universe. It will happen to our earth.

So it was written in the Bible, and modern science has amply served to confirm it: *'All go unto one place; all are of the dust, and all turn to dust again.'* This is a powerful and frightening idea. How shall we respond to it? Can we still hold joy in our hearts? Indeed SciGen has taught us that all things perish but has shown us also that there is an eternal world beyond our full understanding. The eternal and perfect world is just as real as the material world that confounds us. Do not limit yourself to what you can see with your eyes. Tap into the energy and possibility that eternity provides. This is the power of the Spirit, for it is written: *'For he shall not much remember the days of his life; because God answereth him in the joy of his heart.'*

SciGen has shown us the frightening nature of this world, that the material world is transitory. At the same time, SciGen provides us with a glimpse of the eternal. Science has revealed to us a perfect world where logic and simplicity lie beneath the chaos we see with our eyes. Science has shown us there is an unseen world connected in some mysterious way to the seen world. Faith is also of this other, unseen world. Faith is not subject to the corruption and impermanence of the world we see. As we align ourselves with our faith, we align ourselves with a perfect and eternal reality. For it is written: *'The just shall live by his faith.'* We must pray for our faith, for we cannot reach faith on our own.

The seen world is transitory and impermanent: *'I have seen all the works that are done under the sun; and behold, all is vanity and a chasing after wind.'* The unseen world, just as real, is where faith brings us and where in faith we must dwell.

'By the word shall ye be saved'

What is the salvation of man? Salvation comes from our release from the shackles of this world and our connection to the eternal world. Salvation is awareness of a world beyond the burdens of this world. Salvation is finding joy within our present circumstances, by looking beyond to the eternal. Salvation is a life of hope and possibility in which we naturally find righteousness. How can the word bring us to salvation?

> How does the word bring us to salvation in SciGen? What is salvation in SciGen? Salvation in SciGen is much the same as it is for believers: freedom from the limited potential of the seen world. To be saved in SciGen, we must connect to the eternal unseen world. To do that in SciGen, the only way we know how is to develop our 'spiritual antenna'. We must reorient our minds and increase our sensitivity to ideals and concepts that will propel us towards a richer experience of life. In SciGen, this is but a matter of the *psyche*. Greater spiritual fulfillment within SciGen is a matter of reorienting our thought processes, of reorienting the pattern of neurons firing in our brains. Words can create this realignment. When we read words, we change the physical structure of our brains. These changes in structure can certainly lead to improved thought processes that increase our spirituality. In SciGen, words are powerful tools to reach salvation.

Believers know that words are how the almighty communicates with us. Therefore, His words are sacred. For it is written: *'For it is sanctified by the word of God and prayer.'* We must strive thus: *'to be born again, not of corruptible seed, but of incorruptible, by the word of God, which liveth and abideth for ever.'*

'Do not seek what is right and good by your eyes and ears, but by faith'

Most of us want to do the *right thing*. We seek to justify ourselves by embracing the good. What can the material world teach me about virtue and wisdom? Through science, can I find virtue?

When considering virtue in SciGen, what is lacking is a scientific experiment that tells us what is good and what is evil. *The concepts of good and evil remain outside the purview of science.* Science has revealed to us the existence of eternal worlds and perfect objects. Such majesty is contained within the material world as we understand it today. SciGen brings many blessings, because the material world is an awesome and powerful presence that affects us deeply. SciGen does not bring the blessing of justifying your life, of stamping your life with a seal of approval *that it is a good life*. Yet, you may desperately want to know you are leading a good life. SciGen can only help you understand that you must seek beyond the material world to achieve a justified and fulfilling life. SciGen can point you in a direction, but it will not get you to your destination.

Faith is the only path to your destination. To find fulfillment and a meaningful life, you must exercise faith. Faith is the foundation of a meaningful and purposeful life. There is no other way besides faith.

'Rejoice in the gift of science that has been brought into this world'

Science is the study of the material world. For believers, science is the study of the world that God created. Science is a method for understanding and interacting with the material world. This method has created a treasure trove of information that we can use to make our lives *better*. (We only know what better is through faith.) Science is very young compared to humankind (only a few hundred years old in its modern form), but has already had a profound effect. Science has created a conflict with past doctrines and religious belief. Is this conflict irreconcilable?

Science is a gift. Science was given to us (as everything is given to us) by a higher power. *Rejoice in this gift!* Do not condemn it, for the power of science is a property of man and a property of this world. Science itself is not a sin. Science is a method, based on logic and common sense, and on the application of logic to observations of the world around us. The power of science emanates from this world that has been given to us. *May we use scientific knowledge to do good!* Do not worship science, but worship the higher power that gave science to us. We have only begun to know the treasures that science can provide. *Rejoice!*

'Be not a fool'

This world that has been given to us is ruled by a power far beyond our understanding and control. Our just and right humility teaches us to respect this greatest power in our lives. It is foolishness to ignore or contradict this power. Believers know that God is master of their lives. A life in tune with God is a life lived in respect of God Almighty's awesome power and a search for God's will in our lives. It is foolish to go against God's over-arching plan, for it is written: *'Everyone therefore who hears these words of mine, and does them, I will liken him to a wise man who built his house on a rock...Everyone who hears these words of mine, and doesn't do them, will be like a foolish man who built his house on the sand.'*

In SciGen too, the great over-arching power is *Vahhd*. Only a fool would dream of making plans and taking actions that contradict nature's laws. Such arrogant plans and actions will of necessity lead to disaster. The designer of an aircraft knows that only certain designs will actually fly. Designers and engineers must be learned in the ways of *Vahhd*, which requires hard work and discipline. Such effort is a sign of respect for *Vahhd*. Those who choose to ignore *Vahhd* and the Absolute Truth will pay a heavy price. Yet, people do forget the Absolute Truth and behave like fools, only to have their worlds crash down upon them, because they do not obey the Law that *Vahhd* has put down. It is most often excesses of pride that lead us down the wrong path, ignoring the great power that is *Vahhd*. This happens with material things, and also with our human interactions. We ignore at our peril the laws that govern us and that govern those around us. Great outcomes are truly possible when you act with humility, in direct alignment with *Vahhd* and with knowledge of the ways of *Vahhd*.

For it is written:

No one can serve two masters…You cannot serve both God and Mammon. Therefore, I tell you, don't be anxious for your life: what you will eat, or what you will drink; nor yet for your body, what you will wear. Isn't life more than food, and the body more than clothing? See the birds of the sky, that they don't sow, neither do they reap, nor gather into barns. Your heavenly Father feeds them. Aren't you of much more value than they?

Indeed, *Vahhd* feeds the birds by creating the ecology and the environment by which birds can feed themselves for many generations. The birds have no concept of how to create a favorable environment for themselves, yet *Vahhd* does it for them. How we differ from birds is that we can understand the environment and determine when it is becoming a threat and what we must do to overcome that threat. To overcome the threat, our plans must align with *Vahhd*. This cannot be done by serving man alone, but also with humility serving *Vahhd*. Therein lies the path to success and fulfillment.

Words to Live By:

Everything we have is given to us.

Pray.

Every day, give thanks.

Forgive.

Have no excesses of pride, but rather live your life with humility.

Pray for wisdom.

And count this blessing also: that temptation has not found you.

Nothing I have learned has convinced me to be less than
generous, and less than loving.

Deepest joy comes not through the eyes and ears, but through the
spirit.

What does it profit a man to gain the world and lose his soul?

You will know the truth, and the truth will make you free.

In your faith you will find the path of righteousness.

Treat others as you would wish them to treat you.

All things of this world shall perish; yet faith endures.

By the word shall ye be saved.

Do not seek what is right and good by your eyes and ears, but by
faith.

Rejoice in the gift of science that has been brought into this world.

Be not a fool.

7

Embracing the Infinite

I hope this little book has brought you comfort. We live in a world full of pain, conflict and anguish. We want peace and understanding, which seem so difficult to find. I have shared my journey with you. I hope that after reading this book you find a measure of peace and understanding.

What are the next steps? How can you truly 'embrace the infinite'? The answer comes with knowing the truth of this world. Embracing the infinite means understanding the powerful roles of the seen and unseen in our lives.

You want to lead a better life. I recommend that you use the ideas and words presented in this book. Meditate on the word. Meditate on the seen and unseen in your life. By reflection and action, try to become closer to the truth and to the eternal in your life. Do not live your life solely with a focus on material things. Let eternal truths inform your decisions. Most important, acknowledge the power that principles and ideas have in your life. The unseen affects you directly. Acknowledge the power that attitude has in your life. Acknowledge also the mystery of your being alive.

We humans are beings with a special awareness of, and sensitivity to, the unseen. Rejoice in this gift and reflect upon how the unseen world affects you directly. We discount the unseen too easily and don't recognize its enormous influence in our lives. Finding true fulfillment is intangible, yet we can achieve it. Do not be afraid to acknowledge that you depend on that which cannot be measured, counted or precisely defined. Such is a mystery of life. There is the power of the measurable and the power of the unmeasurable. Both powers are great.

Everything physical will decay. Everything you see with your eyes will eventually be gone. Yet eternal and perfect things *are* in this world. This is a profound mystery. Give thanks for this truth.

You know that to reach true fulfillment you must go beyond science. Know that prayer is the foundation of fulfillment. Prayer will bring you closer to the truth and closer to the mystery of your own being. Move forward in your life through prayer.

Find your favorite words from Chapter 6 and make them part of your life. Write down these words and place them somewhere where you can see them every day. When you rise in the morning or sleep at night, meditate upon the words. Understand why these words are true and why they affect you.

You can be what you most dream of. It requires faith. You can scale the mountain and reach the highest peaks, but only faith will get you there. If man has any hope, he must live by faith.

And yet, 'Be not a fool!' Do not fool yourself into thinking that faith alone is your path to the deepest fulfillment. Industry and diligence are important also. *Vahhd* is a great power that rules all. There are ways that *Vahhd* is understandable to us. Use the gift of your conscious mind to make decisions that do not contradict *Vahhd*. Be aware of *Vahhd*'s power as you go forward.

Life is a spiritual journey. Do not focus on material things alone. Strive to nurture your soul with the unseen. Where are you now and what does it mean to you? Where are you going next? When you reach your next destination, what will that mean to you? Get there. Pray for understanding and wisdom – the answers are there but you must seek them.

If you are humble and pray, you will find *Vahhd* is your guardian angel. You must acknowledge *Vahhd*'s power and use diligence and industry to understand *Vahhd*. If you are on the right side of *Vahhd*, *Vahhd* will protect you. If you mock *Vahhd* or taunt *Vahhd* with lies, then *Vahhd* will strike you down. *Vahhd* can raise you or destroy you, but you cannot choose which. *Vahhd* will do what *Vahhd* will do. Strive to know *Vahhd* and ask for guidance. *Vahhd* blesses those who are pure of heart.

Embrace the infinite that surrounds you. Recapture your sense of awe. All that we have is given to us. There is a greater power than you. Accept it and do not fear. Your fate is sealed and you will learn it. Embrace your fate and the blessings that have been provided for you.

Give unto others as you would have them give unto you. Forgive as you wish for forgiveness. Admit your sins, and the world will welcome you with renewed friendship.

Judge not, but be the bearer of hopeful tidings. Do not put down your brother but exalt him and his acts, for he too is a child of God. Open your heart to the goodness within each of us and understand your brother's pain. His pain is your pain also, for you are as sticks bound into a bundle. Where your brother goes, there you will go also.

Do not despair, for God loves you. God knows you and endows you with spirit. Do not violate this blessing with wrongdoing.

Pray for yourself and pray for all. Ask for strength and wisdom. Ask for guidance and love and these shall be granted, for the kingdom of heaven is within your reach.

Count the blessings you are given and do not squander them. Live with purpose. Live in joy. Do not make the world small but know its boundlessness. Know the truth and know the joy of the spirit.

Do not fear death but embrace it as God's will. The will of the almighty cannot be shaken nor will the almighty show us our fate. Wait your turn with a peaceful but longing heart. Love the fate that God provides for you.

The spirit shall move you and the spirit shall move mountains. Do not be afraid to proclaim your love of the spirit that protects you and makes you whole.

The truth shall make you whole. By truth shall you truly live. Your vexations are but illusions that divert your path. Find your path by prayer and contemplation. Find your path in righteousness. By truth shall you find the ways to righteousness.

There is one true purpose to life: to serve God. That is, to embrace the infinite. Anything else is vanity.

The Importance of Attitude

We should acknowledge the importance of *attitude* when considering spiritual renewal. Just as *Vahhd* rules all of the material world, so does attitude profoundly affect the spiritual. Attitude is *not* a material object or thing. Attitude is not subject to scientific analysis. Yet, it is the key to spiritual fulfillment.

I illustrate the importance of attitude with the following story:

A young woman, full of promise for her life, sets out on her journey. She climbs mountains and fords large rivers and faces numerous tests of her skills and patience. She successfully overcomes obstacle after obstacle and remains steadfast in pursuit of her goals. She faces and overcomes the obstacles with equanimity and quiet determination. When her destination is close, within reach, she encounters a swindler. The swindler convinces her to lend him one of her prized possessions. After a few days, she realizes he has vanished with her cherished possession. She is devastated. She now has two choices: to become angry and bitter or to refocus on her dreams.

She does not waste time on anger, for she says: 'I have spent my life facing and meeting challenges. I overcome them, because I believe in myself and I believe in God's love. Why should this be different? When I reach a stream, I cross it. When I find a mountain in my path, I climb to the other side. The swindler is no different from any other challenge I have faced in my life, such as the river or the mountain. I do not get angry at the mountain, because I accept it as it is. The mountain is not there to frustrate me, but it is part of the natural order of things. This is also true for the swindler. I do not like it, but the swindler is just living out his true nature. He does not understand the price he is paying for who he is. I am not happy about the swindler, but I am not angry either. I accept that there are rivers and mountains and swindlers. I accept the nature of things as they are.'

The young woman (of wisdom far beyond her years!) has found the true path. Her spiritual nature provides her with great strength and resiliency. Her spirituality is fully compatible with SciGen. In SciGen, we know that the swindler is living out what *Vahhd* has ordained for him. We should seek to protect ourselves from swindlers (as we protect ourselves from the cold and the rain) but neither should we become bitter and angry if the swindler takes advantage. We do not waste time with anger, because the swindler is simply part of the landscape, one of the challenges that life presents to each of us. As we do not become angry at mountains, neither should we become angry at swindlers. We pray for guidance and move forward.

This story shows us *the importance of attitude*. The young woman will lead a happy and fulfilling life because she has the right attitude about the obstacles she faces. Becoming angry in the face of obstacles is counter-productive. Rising to the challenge is a better way. Our reaction to challenges depends on our attitude. Consider these two obstacles: the swindler and the mountain. We react differently to them because of how we have been taught. However, in SciGen, there is no reason to react differently. Mountains, trees and natural obstacles are made of the same stuff as people (including swindlers). This is an example of how SciGen creates a worldview of great unity: we are as mountains or rivers. We come from dust and return to dust.

One can imagine that the great spiritual leaders of the past may have stumbled upon the SciGen worldview. These past leaders did not know what science was. Even so, perhaps they began to wonder if, in reality, mountains and trees and other natural objects were not so different from people. Within SciGen, we know just how similar these things are. These past leaders did not know about science, but they might have guessed about the unity of all things. This unity brings a deeper spiritual understanding and connection to God.

We should not take this perspective to an extreme. Yes, science teaches us about the great unity of all things on this earth.

Everything we see (including us!) is made up of electrons, protons and neutrons. Of course, differences between people and things are substantial. Your own beliefs inform you of how important the differences are between people and things. The unity of SciGen does encourage us to consider a unifying view, and with this view may come a different attitude. Let's return now to the importance of attitude.

What exactly is attitude? Attitude determines how you react to events, things and people around you. Attitude determines the thoughts you will have as you move through life. Attitude can infuse you with great enthusiasm about your life, or cause you to be negative about your life. A difference in attitude between two people can cause them to think completely differently about the *same thing*. There is almost always more than one way to look at something. Attitude determines which point of view you will adopt. We've all known people who seem very negative, because their attitude causes their thoughts to dwell on many negative aspects of their lives. A positive attitude causes our thoughts to be positive. For example, great misfortune may befall you (a car accident). You might think about how unlucky you are (your limb was severed) or how lucky you are (you survived and are still alive).

Attitude and spirituality are closely linked. Attitude is key to improving your spiritual awareness and to making spirituality work for you. The reason for the link between attitude and spirituality is that both are tied to the unseen world. Let's explore another example about attitude: Imagine two people rising in the morning preparing to go to work. Both have similar jobs and incomes, and their lives are largely similar and 'typical'. The first person, on going to his job, reflects on how fortunate he is to have a job. The job is not his favorite, but it gives him a living and numerous opportunities to accomplish something constructive. He realizes that the income his job provides is what feeds him and he knows how very lucky he is to eat well. He is very grateful that the job allows him to thrive. He makes the most of his situation even though it's not the best job in the world, nor the highest income he might aspire to.

The second person has a similar job and situation to the first person, but he has very different thoughts. This second person often thinks about all the things he does not like about his job. He ruminates upon the fact that he has to work in the first place: what a pain that is! There are others who are not so burdened as he. Why is he the unlucky one? What will a lifetime of toil ultimately get him? Although the second person realizes he is better off with a job than without one, he is very aware that there are many who have better jobs than he, making more money. His job is taking advantage of him, not the other way around. He views his job as a tremendous burden that grinds him down and makes his life miserable.

These two people have very different attitudes about their work and lives. Which person is happier? Obviously the first person is happier, the one with a positive attitude. Why doesn't the second person adopt a more positive attitude? There could be many reasons, but SciGen tells us that the second person may be limited in his ability to change his attitude. Attitude emanates from the brain, its physical structure and patterns of neurons. The second person, even if he could, has no awareness of how to change those neuronal patterns to produce more 'happiness' and a better attitude. How does he create the 'happy' neuronal patterns? He likely has no clue.

Now let's try to understand the link between attitude and spirituality. They are different but related. We can define attitude and spirituality as follows: *Attitude* determines the thoughts that occur in our minds as we react or respond to the material world around us, to the situations we find ourselves in.[1] *Spirituality* determines the thoughts in our minds as we react and respond to the unseen world.

Attitude and spirituality are thus linked by the fact that they have to do with how our thoughts evolve based on the seen (attitude) or based on the unseen (spirituality). We are encouraged to believe that, just as spiritual growth is within reach, we can learn to orient our attitudes towards the positive.

An improved attitude opens up a world of new possibilities. Ponder the example we described earlier: the woman overcoming her unfortunate interaction with a swindler. Developing a positive attitude and viewpoint keeps her on a happy and productive path, despite her misfortune. The essence of improved attitude is training your mind to consider several alternative ways of viewing your situation and the world around you. As you learn to consider alternative viewpoints that are positive, so will you be able to consider alternative viewpoints as regards your spiritual nature. That leads to spiritual growth: an improved understanding of and connection to the unseen world.

Let's discuss some examples of spiritual growth and attitude improvement. One pattern we all must face is the 'better than' pattern. We have all been in situations in which we try as hard as we can but fail to perform up to our expectations. We are forced to confront the fact that others, perhaps close to us, have done better than us in an activity or task. A negative way to view this situation is to focus on our shortcomings: how much worse we are than that other person. Focusing on how much worse we are obscures our positive attributes. We may also succumb to 'trashing' ourselves: constantly reminding ourselves of the ways we are deficient.

What is a positive attitude we can adopt in this case? It is that we tried our best (assuming that we did, which we should have). If you try your best but fail to reach your goal, you know you are living up to your potential. According to SciGen, your ultimate potential is beyond your control. Your ultimate potential is given to you; you cannot determine it. As long as you tried your best, you are not responsible for the shortcomings that befall you. *In such situations, your successes and shortcomings are determined by Vahhd, not by you.*

In any situation where you might not reach your goal, the decision you need to make is how hard you will try to reach higher. Although you cannot exceed your potential no matter how hard you try, you can come closer to reaching your potential by dedication, commitment and hard work. We never know exactly what our potential is. We learn more about our potential by expending effort and reaching higher. Deciding to strive higher and reach our potential is something we can actively embark upon. We can consider our shortcomings in a constructive way, to learn how we can improve. We can thus move closer to reaching our potential.[2] We are enlightened and strengthened by a reason to strive for excellence. Our attitude should be to find a constructive and inspiring reason to reach higher. Our spirituality is a tool we can use to reach this result.

Changing your attitude takes effort. You must first break old habits that form from negative thinking. You will have to increase awareness of the role that your attitude plays in your life. You will need to understand how negative perspectives are entering your thoughts. You must develop an ability to create new points of view that are constructive and positive. You will need to develop the habit of thinking positive thoughts in reaction to situations around you. All this is possible if you commit yourself to the goal of improving your attitude.

The unity of all things that SciGen teaches us may promote within you a different attitude. SciGen may help you see things in a new way. This 'new way' will lead you to have different thoughts. These new thoughts are like a wellspring that you can draw upon to improve your attitude and your life. Good things will happen on your spiritual side. SciGen will refresh your spirit if you learn how to think in a new way.

The Importance of Humility

In SciGen, natural law stands above all. There is never a time or moment, not even a microsecond, when natural law is violated. *We are all beholden to it!* We are beholden to *Vahhd* at all times and in every circumstance. Because of this, we might say that *we are all slaves to Vahhd*.

Humility in the face of this enormous, ever-present power is a reasonable reaction and response. Worship of such an enormous, ever-present power is comforting and affirming.

Ignoring the fact that an enormous force stands far above you is fraught with danger. We cannot have everything that we might want or imagine. Everything that happens does so within the limits set by *Vahhd*. Attempting to defeat or circumvent *Vahhd* is sheer folly.

Let us illustrate a humble spirit with the following example:

A man has been born into a good family and been given many advantages in life. He has received a fine education and been blessed with a nimble mind that takes advantage of that education. He expects to lead a successful life.

One day, a thought enters his mind that leads him to start a business. Using knowledge he has gained from great teachers who have taught him, and his own 'self-teaching' also, he sets up the business with a good foundation that allows the business to prosper and grow. Along with friends and colleagues running the business, the business achieves great success and our man becomes wealthy. He believes that he will never want for material things of this world.

One beautiful autumn day, our man ponders his great success and feels truly humbled by it. He knows that his talent and hard work have led to this success. Yet he also knows that he has been blessed with the talent and ability to work hard. Not everyone has been so blessed. Where his qualities have come from he does not fully understand. He bows his head and gives thanks for the blessings he has received, not only because of his own talent and dedication, but from the efforts of those he was worked with and who have worked for him. His success has certainly depended on the right behavior of those he has associated with. His heart is overcome with a feeling of gratitude. He knows deep in his heart that there are powers greater than himself that have led to his success.

What this example shows us is how humility and great success can be companions to each other. In fact, they should go together. To lose humility when success is yours is to forget the Absolute Truth. To forget the Absolute Truth is to banish *Vahhd* from your thoughts. This is done at great peril.

The spiritual lesson that SciGen provides us is: there is a power greater than you. Attempts to go against this power will fail and likely bring you harm. This is a moral lesson also. You will become more moral when you realize there is a *principle* greater than you. Doing the *right thing* is more important than a temporary advantage of material gain.

Yet, in our minds, using our imagination, we can contemplate a world where *Vahhd* is not dominant. That is the where our imagination hurts us rather than helps us. We might revel in the pride of our accomplishments or revel in our victories. Our successes may lead us to think that we have great powers – to accomplish, to win, to excel, to control the world around us. Yet, SciGen teaches us that these powers are given to us – given to us by *Vahhd*. Falling victim to our imaginations, and focusing on our perceived greatnesses, leads us astray. We may well forget the limits of our powers. We may forget that we have received blessings.

Humility is what binds us to the truth of this world. Humility allows us to know who and what we truly are.

Two entities stand in distinct contrast. First, there is the *I*, our image of ourselves, our human personality. In contrast, there is *Vahhd*, the ever-present, all-pervading power that governs all things (according to SciGen). Whereas the *I* is built upon patterns that are manifested in our brains, *Vahhd* is a transformative power that acts upon the material world. There is no question as to which is the greater of these: for *Vahhd* is the greater one.

Woe unto him that does not recognize and worship the powers that stand above him! The more personal power you believe you have, the more risk that you will ignore the power of *Vahhd*. Therefore, be humble. Humility will launch your spirit towards the higher power. Humility will align your attitude with that which is true in this world. Humility is not weakness but strength. With humility, you will find truth. With truth as your guiding light, your power will multiply one thousand times.

Bind your humility to prayer, praying that you may continue your success through the gifts that *Vahhd* bestows upon you. Prayer produces the good works that humility allows. Your humble spirit will soar to new heights. Prayer will create the path to achieve those heights. You shall stand next to God's right hand, doing works that are good in His eyes. This is not possible if your soul is not a humble one. For God knows who the arrogant ones are.

Humility will not deter you from greatness. Be great, as greatness is God's will and destiny for you. God may indeed endow you with great talents. Do not squander them. These talents are the blessings in your life. Acknowledge these blessings. Through diligence and effort, bring to fruition the talents that God provides. Yet, be humble as you receive the gifts that God provides for you.

8

The Mystery

In this book, I have occasionally alluded to a deep mystery that touches everything we do. This mystery is the paradox of 'free will'. In this chapter, I will describe this paradox, but I will not be able to resolve it. I will only be able to introduce the concept and discuss why free will remains a fundamental mystery in our lives.

The paradox of free will arises when our perceptions of ourselves clash with SciGen, the scientific worldview. According to SciGen, everything that happens in our world is based on natural law. Natural law governs the behavior of atoms, molecules and the forces between them. The scientific knowledge that relates to these small 'particles' is known as 'quantum mechanics'. You can think of quantum mechanics as the scientific foundation of the material world. Quantum mechanics is a well-defined theory that allows us to predict how atoms and molecules behave. In SciGen, the human brain is viewed as a part of the material world. The laws of quantum mechanics apply there also.

Therein lies the paradox of free will. My body and its actions have two masters: free will and the rule of natural law. For example, I can will my arm to move up and down. Do it for yourself now, as an example. According to SciGen, your arm moved up and down because signals were sent from your brain to contract your muscles. Your brain sent those signals because something within your brain caused those signals to be sent. The cause has to do with neurons, which are made of molecules. Molecules obey the laws of quantum mechanics, exclusively, all the time. There are no exceptions. *Molecules obey the rules of quantum mechanics, and are not governed by our will.*

Your arm moved up and down because your arm obeys physical

law. What about your will? Didn't you will your arm to move up and down just now? Did it move up and down because of natural law or because you willed it? Can there be two reasons why your arm moved up and down?

Maybe there are two reasons your arm moved up and down. Reason 1: you willed it. Reason 2: quantum mechanics and natural law. If these two reasons are not contradictory then we are forced to conclude that our will can change the behavior of molecules in our brains. Your will caused a chain of events in your brain that led to your arm moving up and down. Is this possible?

Yes, it is possible. According to science, your will resides in your brain. Saying that 'my will caused my arm to move' is similar to saying that 'my brain caused my arm to move'. Since our brains are made of molecules, science tells us that molecules in your brain caused molecules in your arm to move. That's not a problem from a scientific perspective.

It *is* a problem from the perspective of 'free will'. Remember, you willed your arm to move. Therefore, you willed the molecules in your brain to send that signal to your arm. Molecules only respond to natural law. Does that mean your 'will' trumped natural law? Is *Vahhd* not the master we thought it was? Is natural law subservient to your will?

Of course not! Nothing 'trumps' natural law! *Vahhd* rules all of the material universe. The way out of this dilemma is to conclude that 'free will' is an illusion. What we think of as 'free will' is really just a manifestation of natural law. Our wills aren't really free, although we think they are. Our free will is just an idea in our heads. What really happens is that everything we think and do is governed by natural law. We have no choice in the matter, because we are made of atoms and molecules. Quantum mechanics rules all, including our so-called 'free' will.

Therein lies the mystery. Science tells us that free will is an illusion. None of us really believes that. None of us truly under-stands the mystery of our own choices.

We need to believe our wills are free because we cannot function without that concept. If free will is an illusion, why do I need to keep making choices? If free will is an illusion, why am I blamed for my bad behavior? If free will is an illusion, why do I care so much about what I do and what others do? If there is no free will in this world, then what is the point of striving? What is the point of trying? What is the point of having goals?

If I believe the scientific worldview, then I behave in contradiction to my beliefs. There is no way out of this paradox. Who we are and how we behave cannot be aligned with what we 'know'. That is the mystery. Why is it that life must be a paradox? Why can't it all 'make sense'? It cannot, if you believe in the scientific worldview. Science forces us to live our lives with a tear in the fabric of our lives. We cannot 'have it all'. Science forces us to admit that we are living a life of contradiction.

On the other hand, if you believe in something beyond the scientific worldview, then you can live a life without contradiction. If *Vahhd* does not rule all, then free will may have a source outside the material world. That resolves the paradox. Free will can truly be free; it is not bound by natural law. Our lives make sense again. If we believe the scientific worldview is not all there is, how we behave is once again aligned with what we know. We are gratified.

In this sense, then, faith and belief in God may provide us with a deep sense of fulfillment. The tear is gone. We can be aligned. We can feel free. If faith is a form of truth, then indeed, *the truth will set you free.*

9

Infinity and Awe

Infinity is an important idea in science. The material world is filled with infinities. The idea of infinity is often needed for mathematical descriptions of natural law. You might say that the concept of infinity is a part of the natural language spoken by *Vahhd*.

It is common to believe that infinity describes objects that are infinitely large. Many believe that the concept of infinity is associated with eternity. However, infinity also exists in small spaces and for limited time-spans. I was captivated as a boy by the idea that 'infinity' does not mean 'infinitely large'. I distinctly remember it this way. Draw a straight line diagonally across a piece of paper. That line has a certain length. It is not infinitely long. Yet, there is an infinity of numbers contained between the two end points of the line. You can think of this line as being part of a road, and you are driving along that road. Suppose you wish to stop somewhere along the road. There are an infinite number of places you could stop. We can assign a number to each place you might stop. The number we'll use is the distance from the beginning of the road. There are an infinite number of places to stop, and therefore an infinite quantity of numbers contained within that road, even though the road itself has a finite length. I was amazed by this seeming contradiction: fitting an infinite number of things within a finite thing.

What does infinity have to do with you and your spirituality? That requires some explanation. We start with the observation that there is an enormous quantity of infinities that continually surround us every day. Even small things embody infinity within their boundaries. The multiple infinities of nature exist within the very room you may be sitting in right now. All these infinities that exist in nature are why nature is *infinitely complex.*

The infinite complexity of nature means that there are infinitely many ways that nature can present itself. By 'ways', I mean configurations. Mountains can be high or low, and everything in between. The winds that blow through the mountains can be weak or strong and all gradations of speed between the extremes. Such gradations apply similarly for the temperature of the air within the mountains. There is an infinity of combinations of mountain heights, wind speeds and temperatures that can arise. As time passes, nature presents particular values of these quantities, choosing from an infinite set of possibilities. These quantities vary in ways that cannot be predicted or understood easily. The numbers representing mountain height, wind speed and temperature don't repeat in any simple way. The relationships between these numbers may appear unpredictable. The lack of predictability is what we call 'complicated'. The infinite set of possible values that nature can present leads to such complexity.

Nature presents possibilities beyond our imagining. We can be certain of this: whatever we are thinking of now, whatever our worries or concerns are at this moment, there is a vast universe of possibilities that stretches beyond us. A glimpse of these possibilities would astound us. There are boundless numbers of experiences and moments that we will never know or fathom, that we cannot touch. Science clearly shows this to be true.

This complexity of nature is directly relevant to our spiritual quest. Fully realizing that there are vast possibilities that lie beyond our reach is a humbling experience. This realization is also a call to action. Our life must extend beyond the immediate physical environment that we can see and touch. Our life must be lived to touch the infinite. There is no other way to do this than by faith and hope.

The Lord said, *'Everyone who has left houses, or brothers, or sisters, or father, or mother, or wife, or children, or lands, for my name's sake, will receive one hundred times, and will inherit eternal life.'* This message is a call to action. It is a call to revolution in our personal lives. The revolution is commitment not to a thing or a person but to a set of ideas. Such commitment is the essential meaning of a life lived in faith.

Science clearly shows us that engaging only with the seen world prevents us from understanding what lies beyond what we can see. What we cannot see, and what we do not experience directly, is infinite in extent. When we commit to the unseen world – the world of faith – we are able to connect with an infinite world. In making that connection, we are closer to the truth. The truth is that there is a vastness that lies beyond our immediate experience. We can only appreciate this truth through faith. There is no other way. *By faith we embrace the infinite.* By embracing the infinite, we are led closer to the truth.

The Lord also said: *'But many will be last who are first; and first who are last.'* This passage means that there are those who are first materially, but they may be lagging spiritually. Those who see themselves as 'first' because of what they own or control are not seeing the big picture. They are closing themselves off to the infinities that surround them. In doing so, they are moving away from truth and away from spiritual fulfillment. Yet faith is the great equalizer: both the pauper and the prince can equally enjoy the fruits of faith. Nay, he who has less materially will find it easier to be fulfilled by faith.

Our capacity for reason and logic gives us enormous power in the face of nature's infinite complexity. This power may lead us to believe that we are god-like in our abilities. Modern science reinforces the perception of mankind's power. Such power can confuse us and make us vulnerable to excesses of pride. Certainly it is true that we possess a genuine power, related to our intellectual abilities. We should not confuse such power with mastery of nature, which we do not have.

Thinking of nature as somehow 'conquered' by our understanding, we lose that sense of awe that only a true appreciation of nature's complexity can provide. As the awe ebbs away, so does the connection to God. A blind and unfounded atheism returns.

To be spiritually aware, we must be aware of the infinities that surround us every moment. With the feeling of awe that comes with that awareness, we begin to sense the handiwork of God.

10

Infinity and Character

Scientists are learning that our infinite world is also infinitely complex, and scientists have developed a new *complexity theory* to understand it. The science of complexity is fairly recent. Before complexity became a subject of scientific attention, the prevailing idea had been that of a predictable and simpler world, embodied in the phrase 'the clockwork universe'.

About 200 years ago, as scientists were learning more about the scientific ideas created by Isaac Newton, scientists and philosophers conceived of a universe that ran 'like clockwork'. The clockwork universe is a highly predictable world governed by the eternal laws of nature. The predictability of the clockwork universe emerged from Newton's theories of how nature behaved. One of Newton's important ideas that scientists still believe is this: that the laws of nature that we observe here on earth apply to the universe as a whole (that is, these laws apply everywhere). This universality principle remains a core tenet of modern science.

Newton developed a theory of *dynamics*, which is the scientific theory of how the natural world changes over time. The Newtonian theory of dynamics is universal: universal natural laws govern how changes occur, and every object in the universe is subject to these laws. When mathematicians and scientists analyzed Newtonian dynamics, they realized a very important fact. That fact is that nature is 'predictable'. Predictability in Newtonian science has a very specific meaning, which arises thus: If the universe could be known exactly as it is right now, then what the universe will be in the future could be known also. This is the meaning of 'clockwork' in the phrase 'the clockwork universe'. The universe (that is, everything in the universe) runs like a giant clock:

once set in motion, it runs in a predictable way. If you have a good clock and it reads 1pm now, you know that in one hour it will read 2pm and you also know exactly what the clock looks like when it reads 2pm. That is how clocks are predictable, and the universe as a whole was viewed similarly.

The religious implications of such predictability were discussed also, because a universe that is so predictable appears to leave little room for the actions of an almighty God. Little did anyone know that science itself would remove this predictability dilemma, although not in a way that aligned with religious belief. Rather, science came to discover two areas where predictability is violated: within the realm of the tiny microscopic atom, and within the realm of larger macroscopic systems that might be as large as the atmosphere surrounding our earth. ('Macroscopic' is the opposite of 'microscopic' and describes the things large enough to see with our naked eyes.) In both these regimes of the very small and very large, scientists now believe that the clockwork universe is not applicable. Perhaps this leaves a little more room for God to dwell among us.

For this book, we are most interested in the spiritual implications of the scientific knowledge that the natural world is not perfectly predictable. Scientists have been vexed by the notion that although they may know perfectly the natural laws that govern all of nature, scientists cannot actually predict how nature will behave in many important cases. This might seem to be a paradox: how is it that scientists understand natural law, yet cannot use that knowledge to predict what will happen? The reason for this paradox is complicated, and highly mathematical. Yet, we can state quite simply that, in the macroscopic world, the origin of the paradox is complexity: nature is so infinitely complex that even understanding nature is not enough to know what nature will do.

Let's focus this down to a specific example: the weather. We've all listened at some time to the weather report to get a prediction of what tomorrow's weather will be. Since about the 1950s, those weather predictions have been generated using computers to calculate what the mathematical laws of nature predict about the future. We all know the forecasts are not perfect. What some do not know is that even if we had computers unimaginably faster than the computers of today, we still could not calculate future weather perfectly. The reason is 'complexity'. The natural laws that govern the weather are so fundamentally complex that even perfect knowledge of the natural laws, and extremely fast computers to calculate, will not permit us to make perfect forecasts. Significant unpredictability is part of the nature of things. This is a discovery that scientists did not realize a hundred years ago.

What are the spiritual implications? For one, it teaches us the limits of SciGen. Even perfect knowledge and perfect computers do not permit us to predict the future. SciGen's predictive powers are limited. The complexity of nature limits our knowledge of what the future will bring and what science can tell us about that future. What that means spiritually is that we must adopt an attitude of acceptance. The ancient texts, although pre-dating the scientific method, also taught us to be humble in the face of God and to accept our fate, the fate that God provides for us. Modern science does not change this situation fundamentally: we have a fate but cannot know what it is. Our spiritual lives must be lived with this fact in mind. Our ability to control the future is limited by the fact that we cannot know it. We must be prepared spiritually for an element of unpredictability and uncertainty about the future. This uncertainty increases our sense of awe about the great power of *Vahhd* that governs our lives.

How People Are

We can learn from the SciGen perspective when it comes to our social and moral world also. Recall the SciGen perspective on human beings and humanity: humans are simply manifestations of complex physical systems. When scientists believed in the clockwork universe, the perspective that humans are physical systems caused scientists to believe in the predictability and rationality of human nature and behavior. At least, they could hope that humans were rational. Psychologists believed that utopian societies could be constructed if people were trained and conditioned to behave 'properly'. The underlying idea is that people are predictable, and exposing them to the 'correct' environment leads to predictable behavioral outcomes.

Modern science provides a different view. The complexity of human beings ensures their unpredictability. Utopian schemes may be impossible to achieve. Yet, knowing this is a good thing because modern utopian schemes pose a significant moral dilemma. Utopian societies can only succeed if human nature is somewhat predictable. Such societies are constructed in a way that takes advantage of predictable human behavior to create a harmonious and stable society. Many have thought this could work. Let's consider the example of a utopian society based on self-interest. Many have believed that a society based on self-interest could be made to work and be stable and harmonious. After all, self-interest is a universal trait: everyone looks out for themselves. Can we build a utopian society that takes advantage of that?

No, in fact we cannot. Even such an apparently reliable principle as 'self-interest' cannot be the foundation of a perfect utopia. Self-interest as a guiding principle for human behavior is strong, but not unimpeachable. Look at the world today. It is clear that many, many people do things to hurt themselves. Sometimes, it is because they did not know better, and genuinely made a mistake, thinking they would be helped by what they did. But there are also many times when the passions of individuals lie elsewhere than their own self-interest. Those passions might be hate, love, fear, or a fervent belief in God, but whatever these passions are, they can cause us to hurt ourselves. There are many such examples in the world today.

The scientific view that people are too complex to be predictable teaches us to accept people for what they are. We must approach human affairs with humility. The moral failing of utopias is that they assign to man far more power than he actually possesses. The history of utopias over the past 100 to 200 years is largely unsuccessful. Utopias are built upon a very shaky foundation, a foundation that assumes people are predictable. To compensate for the weak foundation, utopian societies often become highly repressive and seek to limit freedom of expression. Limiting freedom of expression can inflame passions that cause people to deviate from their expected behavior. Utopia is not, and never will be, easy to achieve.

Interestingly, science has discarded the notion of a 'clockwork universe' that led to utopian thinking. Science teaches very clearly that complex systems such as human beings are highly unpredictable and 'non-linear'. (By non-linearity, we mean that humans behave far differently from the sum of their parts.) Science informs our spirituality by affirming that we cannot construct utopian societies easily or reliably. Rather, a successful way of life is built upon constant striving. Constant vigilance is required to keep us on the right course. We cannot rely on the 'clockwork universe' to get us from point A to point B with minimal deviation. We cannot simply set up the society we want and let it run its course. Rather, we must define a moral code that we want to live up to, and constantly try to reach that higher ground. Science forces us to face the fact that we must choose our values, and choose what we value most. We cannot create a utopian society using the principle of 'set it and forget it'.

We know the path forward will not be easy, either for us or for those around us. But it is better to 'live by the book' of moral beliefs. It is wrong to suppose that moral and just societies will automatically arise if set into motion by a utopian vision. Those who predict that societal ills will be cured by increased scientific knowledge are not understanding the spiritual message nor the science. The future must be as the past has been: follow commandments. One cannot ignore a moral code, for that is all there is to guide us. Without it, there is no reliable way to keep society on track. We must consciously strive for the values we believe in, by faith. We cannot ignore those values, for if we do, those values will perish in our lives. The values we cherish will not simply appear as a consequence of a morally neutral utopian program. Rather we must consciously choose to believe in a moral code and consciously choose to achieve it.

'If ye keep my commandments, ye shall abide in my love; even as I have kept my Father's commandments, and abide in his love.'

Life is a not a journey of tangible things; it is a spiritual journey. Life is a challenge because we cannot predict or control the future. The answer is faith and prayer.

11

The Fundamental Religious Question

The fundamental question for mankind is not: is there a God? Rather, the question is: what is the nature of God? Is God encompassed solely by *Vahhd*, which is natural law? Or is there a more personal connection to God? If so, what is the nature of that connection?

Skeptics would tell us there is no God because God does not speak to us directly. Why must God be hidden and work in 'mysterious ways'? Why doesn't God appear as a great shining light in the sky? Why doesn't God snuff out all human evil and suffering? God does not, therefore there is no God; so say the atheists.

Yet, atheism has a blindness deep within. Atheists *believe* that because we do not experience God as they expect, there is no God. Yes, it is true that God's presence could be more obvious than it is. God could choose a language and form and literally speak to us. The fact that God does not do this is not proof there is no God. Rather, it teaches us something about the nature of God.

God's nature forces us to experience God by faith. This world, God's world, is the context in which we all live. We should not be so bold as to deny God's existence, but rather first we must try to understand God's creation. SciGen teaches us spiritual lessons derived from His creation. We should take heed.

We live in a world not of our own making. Our world is provided to us from outside ourselves. Whatever you call that thing that is outside of us, from which the world does come, it is just a name. I may call it 'God', and you may call it something else. It does not matter. We live in a world that reveals great powers beyond our imagining. We can call it what we will.

What will we do about this 'Absolute Truth'? We can certainly choose to ignore such things, yet we do so at our peril. We do so at our peril *spiritually*. We are aware of so much more when we are aware of the magnificence and majesty of the great power of this world. We may even feel blessed to live alongside this power. We may try to learn lessons from this power. We may try to honor ourselves and our own miraculous natures by paying heed to the power from which we have arisen. We can deny its existence, but denial is not a path to truth and not a path towards joy. We can enjoy the blessings when we heed the power. Or we can deny it, as many have and many will continue to do. Yet, why embrace spiritual emptiness when we can have so much more? Choosing God is a choice we all can make and we can all reap the benefit, despite the pain and suffering that may be in our lives. Do not turn from God, but heed His word and abide by His love. Seek out the Lord. He is waiting for you to find Him.

Notes

2. An Absolute Truth

1   Note that even though science depends on this Truth, science itself does not reveal Absolute Truth. More on this subject later.

2   Well, not always. If I say A = A, then I've made no transformation.

4. The Seen and the Unseen

1   We will not digress here on the scientific definition of mass. Go with your intuitive understanding: something with mass has weight if pulled on by gravity. If an object's mass is zero, it has energy and travels with the speed of light.

7. Embracing the Infinite

1   Attitude could be defined as how we react to the unseen world also, but we are choosing to partition out this aspect of attitude and call it 'spirituality'.

2   The idea that we can choose to improve ourselves is somewhat mysterious within SciGen. I discuss this further in Chapter 8.

BOOKS

Iff Books is dedicated to publishing intelligent (though not necessarily academic) books covering all aspects of philosophy and science.